3rd Workshop on Computational Creativity in Natural Language Generation (CC-NLG 2018)

Tilburg, The Netherlands
5 November 2018

ISBN: 978-1-5108-7757-3

Printed from e-media with permission by:

Curran Associates, Inc.
57 Morehouse Lane
Red Hook, NY 12571

Some format issues inherent in the e-media version may also appear in this print version.

Printed by Curran Associates, Inc. (2019)

For permission requests, please contact the Association for Computational Linguistics at the address below.

Association for Computational Linguistics
209 N. Eighth Street
Stroudsburg, Pennsylvania 18360

Phone: 1-570-476-8006
Fax: 1-570-476-0860

acl@aclweb.org

Additional copies of this publication are available from:

Curran Associates, Inc.
57 Morehouse Lane
Red Hook, NY 12571 USA
Phone: 845-758-0400
Fax: 845-758-2633
Email: curran@proceedings.com
Web: www.proceedings.com

CC-NLG 2018

The 3rd Workshop on

Computational Creativity in Natural Language Generation

Proceedings of the Workshop

5th November 2018
Tilburg University
The Netherlands

Introduction

Welcome to the third edition of the Workshop on Computational Creativity in Natural Language Generation (CC-NLG), collocated with INLG 2018, the International Conference on Natural Language Generation, held in Tilburg, the Netherlands. As a follow-up of CC-NLG 2016 and 2017, this workshop aims to act as a meeting point for researchers with overlapping concerns; those dealing with text generation from a computational creativity perspective, and researchers in natural language generation with an interest in creative aspects.

Computational Creativity is a popular research goal within NLG, and likewise, language based tasks have long been the pursuit of CC researchers. However, projects have been hosted at a wide range of venues across many academic fields, making chances to meet and discuss developments rare. This separation is compounded by differing research focuses: creativity research tends to be less focused on technical issues in natural language generation, and more on issues related to cognition, aesthetics, and novelty; meanwhile, NLG research tends to focus on technical and theoretical aspects of processes, the informativeness of textual content, and readability of output. However, recent progress in both fields is reducing many of these differences — with creativity projects moving more towards robust implementation, and NLG research including stylistics, variation and literary genres such as poetry or narrative. We believe that both areas are now approaching the point where they can mutually benefit from ongoing work, and a discreet venue in which to discuss these overlapping concerns.

These proceedings include a total of six papers, five focused on narrative generation and storytelling, and one on riddle generation. These were chosen from ten submitted papers, each reviewed by three members of the program committee. In addition to presentation of papers, the workshop in Tilburg will host an invited talk by Pablo Gervás and an open discussion on Computational Creativity in Natural Language Generation.

Finally, we would like to thank everyone who contributed to the success of this workshop, especially the authors, the program committee members, the organisers of the INLG 2018 conference and the INLG 2018 workshop chairs.

Hugo Gonçalo Oliveira, Ben Burtenshaw, Raquel Hervás

Organizers

Workshop Chairs:

Hugo Gonçalo Oliveira, University of Coimbra
Ben Burtenshaw, University of Antwerp
Raquel Hervás, Universidad Complutense de Madrid

Program Committee:

Amílcar Cardoso, University of Coimbra
Carlos León, Universidad Complutense de Madrid
Cyril Labbé, Université Grenoble Alpes
Ehud Reiter, University of Aberdeen
Emiel Krahmer, Tilburg University
Folgert Kasdorp, Meertens Instituut, Royal Dutch Academy of Arts and Sciences
François Portet, Université Grenoble Alpes
Gonzalo Méndez, Universidad Complutense de Madrid
Hannu Toivonen, University of Helsinki
Manuel Portela, University of Coimbra
Matthew Purver, Queen Mary University of London
Mike Kestemont, University of Antwerp, Belgium
Pablo Gervás, Universidad Complutense de Madrid
Rafael Pérez y Pérez, Universidad Autónoma Metropolitana at Cuajimalpa
Tony Veale, University College Dublin

Table of Contents

Conference Programme

Monday, 5th November

	9:00–10:50 Session 1
9:00–9:10	Short introduction: *A Brief Introduction to Natural Language Generation within Computational Creativity* Ben Burtenshaw
9:10–10:00	*Content determination strategies for narrative: real-life reporting vs. fiction* (Invited Talk) Pablo Gervás
10:00–10:15	*Seeking the Ideal Narrative Model for Computer-Generated Narratives* Mariana Ferreira and Hugo Gonçalo Oliveira
10:15–10:30	*Discourse Embellishment Using a Deep Encoder-Decoder Network* Leonid Berov and Kai Standvoss
10:30–10:50	*Exploring Lexical-Semantic Knowledge in the Generation of Novel Riddles in Portuguese* Hugo Gonçalo Oliveira and Ricardo Rodrigues
10:50–11:30	Coffee break
	11:30–12:30 Session 2
11:30–11:50	*Content Determination for Chess as a Source for Suspenseful Narratives* Richard Doust and Pablo Gervás
11:50–12:05	*Generating Stories Using Role-playing Games and Simulated Human-like Conversations* Alan Tapscott, Carlos León and Pablo Gervás
12:05–12:30	Final discussion

Invited Talk

Content determination strategies for narrative: real-life reporting vs. fiction By Pablo Gervás, Universidad Complutense de Madrid.

The crucial role of narrative in human communication has two different modes. Narrative is often used to report events extracted from our experience of real life that we want other people to know about. At other times, narrative is used to convey entirely fictional set of events that have been put together for the purpose of entertaining or exercising our sensibility. Although the surface forms of the discourses created in each of these modes are fundamentally similar, the content determination strategies employed during composition present significant differences. Whereas in one case the process is mainly one of selection, in the other there is likely to be a large percentage of invention. Yet both the selection and the invention are likely to be guided or informed by considerations of narrative structure and successful narrative outcomes. The talk will describe recent work on computational modelling of these two narrative modes and present insights arising from their joint consideration into a single framework capable of switching from one to the other (and considering hybrid modes of operation) much as humans are seen to do.

A Brief Introduction to Natural Language Generation within Computational Creativity

Ben Burtenshaw
Computational Linguistics & Psycholinguistics Research Center, and
The Antwerp Centre for Digital Humanities and Literary Criticism
The University of Antwerp, Prinsstraat 13, Antwerp, Belgium
benjamin.burtenshaw@uantwerpen.be

Abstract

This paper is an introduction to The 3rd Workshop on Computational Creativity in Language Generation (CC-NLG 2018), collocated with The 11th International Conference on Natural Language Generation (INLG 2018). The workshop acts as an overview of projects from the Computational Creativity field present within the general field of Natural Language Generation, and references further reviews within the area. Accepted papers to the workshop will use contemporary NLG methods or approach NLG problems from a creative perspective. The workshop intends to showcase creative applications as a worthwhile and meaningful pursuit to other NLG researchers.

1 Introduction

This short paper will introduce the workshop Computational Creativity in Natural Language Generation (CCNLG), and point to a limited portion of the field that surrounds it. CCNLG is intended as a discussion of recent advancements within Computational Creativity (CC) that are relevant to the field of Natural Language Generation (NLG), or utilize NLG methods. Collocated with The International Conference on Natural Language Generation (INLG), it also attempts to showcase how creative applications can utilise innovative NLG methods toward novel applications. This paper acts as brief introduction for researchers from outside the CC field.
Language has sat at the core of CC research since the field's origins. NLG projects by Meehan, Gervas, Colton, and Veale are key examples of CC, as well as methodological cornerstones to researchers finding their way in a theoretically nuanced arena. In turn, language generation projects have become key reference points to CC researchers working in other application areas. In short, Computational Creativity within Natural Language Generation is by no means an underdeveloped research trajectory; however, research comes from a broad range of venues and events, and there is a lack of discussion for concerns specific to the field itself. Conferences that have hosted CCNLG research include, INLG, The conferences of the Association for Computational Linguistics (ACl, nAC-ACL, EACL), the International Conference on Computational Creativity (ICCC), as well as its predecessor workshops at ECAI, IJCAI, ECCBR and ICCBR, various AISB symposia on creativity and poetry, Computational models of Narrative workshop, International Conference on Interactive Digital Storytelling, the Intelligent Narrative Technologies workshop series. In recent years NLG has become relevant to the general public through creative application in dialogues systems, chatbots, and twitter bots. These widely available tasks have thrown creative language generation into the public eye, opening up a broad base of possible users. Typically though, NLG has been used by CC researchers in three formal areas; story generation, poetry generation, and joke generation. That said, CC researchers have used NLG in many applications from recipe to lyric generation. As well as introducing application within CC in NLG, this paper will also reference relevant literature reviews that support the workshop.

2 Story Generation

Stories are a fundamental part of creative writing, and have been generated by CC researchers for decades [3]. Furthermore, narratives are a crucial part of language outside of formal stories, and re-

Proceedings of the 3rd Workshop on Computational Creativity and Natural Language Generation, pages 2–4,
Tilburg, November 2018.

searchers have used NLG to produce informal stories [4].

An early example of creative story generation is TALE-SPIN, which generated Aesop's Fables based on the user's input (Meehan, 1977). The user was asked a series a questions during creation, that TALE-SPIN combined with prior knowledge on story attributes to generate a tale. The user could also chose from a set of morals, like "never trust flatterers", which the system would then attempt to communicate through the story. In essence, TALE-SPIN was a goal based problem solving system, that saw the attributes of the proposed Aesop fable as a problem, that it could solve via the inclusion of the correct knowledge pieces in a story. Also using a knowledge based approach, Universe by Michaeal Lebowitz draws on a database of character definitions and plot outlines to create stories around a user proposed theme [10]. McIntyre and Lapata developed one of the first search-based narrative systems that used user-input to search a database for relating phrases [12]. Gervas 2009 gives a detailed overview of story generation advancements from 1974 to 2009 [8].

3 Poetry Generation

Poems are an important part of how humans use language to be creative. Outside of formal poetry, from metaphor to analogy, poetic language litters our public and personal communication. The earliest examples of autonomous poetry can be traced back to Oulipo's lo-fi assemblages of text from existing poems. But it is with Manarung, Gervas, and Colton at the turn of the century that systems used fundamentally poetic properties, like rhyme and meter, to move beyond the experimental and arbitrary combination of language [5, 7, 11]. For an expanded review of poetry generation, look to Gonçalo Oliveira 2017 [9].

4 Joke Generation

Joke generation has been one of the most fervent areas of NLG within CC. Researchers initially focused on pun generation, where knowledge intensive protocols were used to align contrary antitheses and comparisons (Binsted and Ritchie, 1994; Shah, 2016)[1, 13]. In more recent years researchers have moved on to broader and more sophisticated levels or humoristic language, where structure is less forgiving [2, 13]. Also falling under joke generation, Oliveira's meme generator exploits the formalities of the medium within a working system.[9]. For a survey of joke generation, look to Section 6 of Gatt and Krahmer's 2017 book chapter, which is also a valuable study of NLG more broadly, and highlights the value in connections between CC and NLG [6].

5 Conclusion

CCNLG is a recently initiated workshop within the shifting field of NLG, that serves to expose macro trajectories for creative projects, and discuss their merit on formal and theoretical levels. At a juncture of two fields, CCNLG sits in a challenging yet interesting location, where researchers can take advantage of a broad set of innovative methods and perplexing applications. However, the end tasks – joke, story, or poetry generation – hold established bodies of literature and rich histories; it is therefore crucial that we are aware of this work as we look forward.

References

[1] Kim Binsted and Graeme Ritchie. "An Implemented Model of Punning Riddles". In: *Proceedings of the Twelfth National Conference on Artificial Intelligence*. AAAI. Seattle, Washington: AAAI Press, 1994, pp. 148–160. ISBN: 978-0-262-51078-3.

[2] Kim Binsted et al. "Computational Humor". In: *IEEE Intelligent Systems* 21.2 (2006), pp. 59–69. ISSN: 1541-1672. DOI: 10.1109/MIS.2006.22. URL: https://www.research.ed.ac.uk/portal/en/publications/computational-humor(4837fac1-cffa-4d55-b456-1691a4db2308)/export.html (visited on 09/16/2018).

[3] C. Callaway and J. Lester. "Narrative Prose Generation". In: *Articial Intelligence* 139.2 (Aug. 2002), pp. 213–252. DOI: https://www.sciencedirect.com/science/article/pii/S0004370202002308?via%3Dihub. URL: https://pdfs.semanticscholar.org/0013/586baf188dd9d6b0408f540b808053a76a61.pdf.

Proceedings of the 3rd Workshop on Computational Creativity and Natural Language Generation, pages 2–4, Tilburg, November 2018. ©2018 Association for Computational Linguistics

[4] Yun-Gyung Cheong and R. Michael Young. "Narrative Generation for Suspense: Modeling and Evaluation". In: *Joint International Conference on Interactive Digital Storytelling*. Springer, 2008, pp. 144–155. URL: http://link.springer.com/chapter/10.1007/978-3-540-89454-4_21 (visited on 01/24/2017).

[5] Simon Colton, Jacob Goodwin, and Tony Veale. "Full-FACE Poetry Generation". In: *Proceedings of the Third International Conference on Computational Creativity*. 2012, pp. 95–102. URL: http://computationalcreativity.net/iccc2012/wp-content/uploads/2012/05/095-Colton.pdf (visited on 02/01/2017).

[6] Albert Gatt and Emiel Krahmer. "Survey of the State of the Art in Natural Language Generation: Core Tasks, Applications and Evaluation". In: (Mar. 29, 2017). arXiv: 1703.09902 [cs]. URL: http://arxiv.org/abs/1703.09902 (visited on 10/16/2018).

[7] Pablo Gervás. "An Expert System for the Composition of Formal Spanish Poetry". In: *Knowledge-Based Systems* 14.3-4 (June 2001), pp. 181–188. ISSN: 0950-7051. DOI: 10.1016/S0950-7051(01)00095-8. URL: https://doi.org/10.1016/S0950-7051(01)00095-8 (visited on 09/11/2018).

[8] Pablo Gervás. "Computational Approaches to Storytelling and Creativity". In: *AI Magazine* 30.3 (2009), p. 49. URL: http://www.aaai.org/ojs/index.php/aimagazine/article/viewFile/2250/2101 (visited on 07/13/2017).

[9] Hugo Gonçalo Oliveira. "A Survey on Intelligent Poetry Generation: Languages, Features, Techniques, Reutilisation and Evaluation". In: *Proceedings of the 10th International Conference on Natural Language Generation*. The 10th International Conference on Natural Language Generation. Santiago de Compostela, Spain: Association for Computational Linguistics, 2017, pp. 11–20. DOI: 10.18653/v1/W17-3502. URL: http://aclweb.org/anthology/W17-3502 (visited on 09/11/2018).

[10] M. Lebowitz. "Story Telling as Planning and Learning". In: Columbia University Computer Science Technical Reports, CUCS-202-85 14.1985 (1986), pp. 483–502. DOI: https://doi.org/10.7916/D8VX0QJZ. URL: https://academiccommons.columbia.edu/doi/10.7916/D8K362MH/download.

[11] Hisar Maruli Manurung. "An Evolutionary Algorithm Approach to Poetry Generation". Edinburgh: University of Edinburgh. College of Science and Engineering. School of Informatics., July 2004. URL: https://www.era.lib.ed.ac.uk/bitstream/handle/1842/314/IP040022.pdf?sequence=1&isAllowed=y.

[12] Neil McIntyre and Mirella Lapata. "Learning to Tell Tales: A Data-Driven Approach to Story Generation". In: *Proceedings of the Joint Conference of the 47th Annual Meeting of the ACL and the 4th International Joint Conference on Natural Language Processing of the AFNLP: Volume 1-Volume 1*. Association for Computational Linguistics, 2009, pp. 217–225. ISBN: 1-932432-45-0.

[13] Priyanshi R Shah. "Computational Creativity: Automated Pun Generation". In: *International Journal of Computer Applications* 140 (2016), p. 5. URL: https://pdfs.semanticscholar.org/8255/d25db977107357f670c132690282164655ed.pdf.

Proceedings of the 3rd Workshop on Computational Creativity and Natural Language Generation, pages 2–4,
Tilburg, November 2018. ©2018 Association for Computational Linguistics

Seeking the Ideal Narrative Model for Computer-Generated Narratives

Mariana Chinellato Ferreira
Center for Portuguese Literature
Materialities of Literature
University of Coimbra, Portugal
mariana.ferreira@student.fl.uc.pt

Hugo Gonçalo Oliveira
Center of Informatics & Systems
Department of Informatics Engineering
University of Coimbra, Portugal
hroliv@dei.uc.pt

Abstract

The aim of this paper is to discuss and sketch an ideal narrative model based on post-classical narratology approaches, namely Cognitive Narratology to help to improve the interestingness of the output in computer-generated narratives. This model will be further tested in a prototype of a generative system in the Portuguese language that will be based on Brazilian urban novels.

1 Introduction

Generative Literature is not novel in Literary nor Computer Science experiments, but there has been an increase of studies focused on this matter lately, both by artists and scientists. For the last few decades, Literary Studies and Computer Science have been crossing paths, which led to the development of the Digital Humanities.

Among other applications, Computational Creativity has been focusing on the issues of creativity and the possibility of programming a computer to produce art or learn how to produce it. In the scope of language, there are various works in collaboration with Linguistics, Stylistics and Literary Studies, especially when analyzing several textual aspects of large text corpora. More complex approaches are used in CC for the development of automatic text generation systems (Kybartas and Bidarra, 2017; Goncalo Oliveira, 2017)

This paper is part of a Ph.D. research that aims to foster the crossover between Literary Studies and Computer Science to contribute to the solution of linguistic, literary and aesthetic issues in computer-generated literary artifacts. To this end, it is necessary to find a more general narrative model to be applied in a prototype of a system that generates literary narratives in Portuguese.

Even though the research intends to use post-classical narratological theories[1], it is hard to work with narratives in Computational Creativity without using any formal model of literary narrative. Ergo this paper focuses on understanding how the systems develop and apply the narrative model, most commonly Propp's Morphology of the Folktale (or any other Formalist or Structuralist approach) and propose a new model that will be further tested on the prototype.

At the current stage of the research, most of the work is still theoretical and must be tested. Nevertheless, the aim of this paper is to present a few systems and show how their narrative is developed, dividing them into systems that use Propp's Morphology as a narrative model and systems that present their own narrative models. The following part of the paper intends to present the proposition of a new narrative model based on Brazilian Urban Novel with the background of the Cognitive Narratology (Herman, 2000).

2 Propp's Morphology of the Russian Folktale

In the introduction of the second edition of the Morphology of the Folktales, Alan Dundes shows the reader the importance of Propp's work and presents several different usages of this theory in multiple study fields. He first states that Propp inspired many formalists and structuralists into de-

[1]Built upon the French Structuralism, Semiotics and Russian Formalism, classical narratology is composed by theories developed by renowned theorists such as Tzvetan Todorov, Gérard Genette, Roland Barthes, Vladimir Propp, Seymour Chatman, Gerald Prince, A.J. Greimas, among others, who tried to find the characteristics of the narrative text to generate a logical structural model of narratives. Post-classical narratology does not criticize the formal models directly, but they suggest the expansion of these models, mainly through the merge of narratology with different study fields to understand narrative beyond its own form. Among the post-classical theorists David Herman (cognitive science), Manfred Jan, Monika Fludernik (conversational narrative), Marie-Laure Ryan (digital), Susan Lanser (genre), among others stand out.

Proceedings of the 3rd Workshop on Computational Creativity and Natural Language Generation, pages 5–10,
Tilburg, November 2018. ©2018 Association for Computational Linguistics

veloping their own theories (Propp, 1968).

Because Propp's morphology was the only work in literature to dissect a literary genre into its smallest parts, a great number of projects on narrative generation – especially the ones that use story grammars (Lakoff, 1972) as its basis – use Propp's model in some way. In fact, his work has always been very useful for the development of several systems that generate narratives automatically. However, its main criticism is in the fact that Propp has never related his model to the Russian social and cultural context[2]. Even though many literary texts and genres seem to be timeless their peculiarities in form and content come mainly from their social and cultural contexts.

Thus, one of the hypotheses this paper takes into consideration is the need to focus on the context of the narrative for the improvement of the narrative model. It does not mean to discard the formalist and structuralist models, but to approach them with the help of post-classical narratological approaches. In this paper, we try to observe the narrative model through the lens of the Cognitive Narratology (Herman, 2013).

3 Narrative Generators

This part of the papers is dedicated to the presentation of different linear narrative generators and their features in terms of literary inspiration. The systems were studied through the written materials found (Ph.D. thesis, papers, reports) once most of the systems are not available to the public.

It is interesting to notice that a considerable number of systems even when they do not present a direct link to Propp's morphology they are somehow related to the fantastic (Todorov, 1975) or in the realm of the folktales. This is an interesting fact that raises some questions about the choice of literary genre to be emulated.

The first obvious reason for the fantastic to be an option for the narrative generation is the fact that there are formal models of these narratives. Another possible reason might be that the fantastic does not need verisimilitude and strange, curious and atypical things are able to occur in the story. And finally, maybe because the creators of the systems simply liked this literary genre.

Regardless of the reason why the fantastic was chosen, it is the most common choice among the most well-known narrative generators as it will be discussed next.

3.1 Systems based on Propp's Morphology

As its name suggests, ProtoPropp uses the Morphology of Folktales as its narratological background as "it provides a simple (and well-known in the field) formal system, something which is unusual to find in other post-structuralist or semiotic narrative theories" (Peinado and Gervás, 2005).

Imababuchi and Ogata (2014) developed a Propp-based story generator that can work independently, generating stories with the structure of Russian folktales, or work as part of an Integrated Narrative System. They pointed out that most Propp-based systems focus on the function while they intend to include "many productive and theoretical ideas to contribute to story generation in various sides" (Imabuchi and Ogata, 2014).

In the introduction of his Ph.D., Turner (1993) tells the reader that he stumbled upon Propp's morphology and thought it was fascinating that he could reduce the folktale into grammar. Although it was his first inspiration, his final computer program barely resembled Propp's grammar. Minstrel (Turner, 1993) is a case-based problem solver system that generates short stories about King Arthur and the Knights of the Round Table, also in the realm of the fantastic and fairy tales.

Brandon Tearse, Noah Wardrip-Fruin and Michael Mateas (2010) studied Turner's Minstrel in order to identify the crucial elements of the system (once it is not available in any format), explore possible new usages of the system, and develop and make available a new version of the system. As there are few theoretical materials about the classical systems as well as few or no access to the systems (or their code) for a deeper analysis, Minstrel Remixed is an important tool for practical analysis of story generation even though it presents a few challenges in terms of usage, especially for those not familiarized with programming. As a development of Minstrel, Minstrel Remixed (renamed Skald) (Tearse et al., 2010) has the same theoretical background.

Even though BRUTUS (Bringsjord and Ferrucci, 1999) generates short narratives with the theme of betrayal, Propp's grammar has some influence in its development once this system produces its stories using story grammars "moving

[2]Different from Propp, Lèvi-Strauss (1955) developed a study on the structure of the myth where he took into consideration their social and cultural context. (Propp, 1968).

Proceedings of the 3rd Workshop on Computational Creativity and Natural Language Generation, pages 5–10,
Tilburg, November 2018. ©2018 Association for Computational Linguistics

from general descriptions of narrative and simple folktales to generating fully realized narratives" (Kybartas and Bidarra, 2017).

3.2 Other narrative models

There are however systems that developed their own narrative model based on different types of literary texts as it follows.

GESTER (Pemberton, 1984) is a plot generator whose grammar is based on Old French epic narratives. Even though it is not based on Propp, epic narratives also present fantastic events and might be somehow similar to folktales (once their origin is from oral tradition). Her work is interesting because she states that "[a] full story generating system would need access to many different kinds of separate but interacting knowledge" (Pemberton, 1989), such as the story structure, the audience, the author, the cultural context and the rules of the sub-genre.

Although MEXICA (Pérez y Pérez, 1999) does not use Propp's morphology or any kind of story grammars, and it tells the story of the Mexicas — old inhabitants of Mexico City. Its output may be classified as fantasy once it presents the love of the princess and the knight, kings and queens, gods and magical ceremonies. Different from other systems, MEXICA worries about characteristics outside the textual form. Among the postconditions (the effects of the primitive actions) there are the emotional links between characters, their tensions and their positions.

Mark Owen Riedl (2004) developed an architecture for the creation of automatic stories that divides the generation process of a narrative into three layers: (1) fabula generation, (2) discourse generation and (3) media representation. The stories are based in fables and fairy tales, as its name suggests and it is indirectly inspired by Propp's morphology and directly by Genette's narrative discourse and Gerald Prince's (1987) dictionary of narrative. It is interesting to notice that his work starts to merge a more contemporary narratological approach by the use of David Herman's and Marie-Laure Ryan's works (both post-classical theorists) with classical narratology.

These are just a few examples out a vast field where it is possible to find many different systems that generate linear or interactive narratives that might use Propp's morphology or not. The systems presented previously meet the purpose of illustrating that there is the predominance use of the proppian model both in story grammars or literary genre (even though there are other systems that do not use folktales as their main literary genre, such as Brutus, Author, Universe, nn, among others).

4 Ideal Narratological Approach

The presentation of the systems shows us that the formalization of the folktales seems to be the first step in the development of new narrative models to be applied in computer-generated narrative systems. From the literary point of view, there seems not to be any other way for us to analyze a literary text of any kind this thoroughly. But it is known, both in computer science and in literature, that the formalist approach has its weaknesses and the main criticism is the reduction of the importance of the historical, biographical, social and cultural context of the text.

In fact, at first, any kind of pure formalization sounds like the best option in terms of developing narratives using a computer. But the need for more humanistic approaches in order to improve the creativity in artistic artifacts automatically generated is also noticed in the field of Computational Creativity (Pérez y Pérez, 2018).

So, this section of the paper intends to present an alternative to the approaches available.

5 Cognitive Narratology

To some degree, formalist and structuralist models were very useful tools in the early stages of Artificial Intelligence and Computational Creativity. As suggested by Pérez y Pérez (2018), the field of Computational Creativity presents a continuum (CC-Continuum) that has two opposite sides: on one side there is the Engineering-Mathematical Approach were scientists work on technical tasks of optimization while on the other side there is the Cognitive-Social Approach where scientist study the human behavior as basis for the development of creative computer artifacts. Their major work is "to find ways of representing in computer terms relevant cognitive, cultural and social behaviours" (Pérez y Pérez, 2018).

As Literary Theories are too subjective to be implemented in a computer system, it is important to maintain a certain level of formality learnt from Propp's morphology. So, we propose to merge the propian approach to the Cognitive Narratology, once it supports the structure of a story world and

Proceedings of the 3rd Workshop on Computational Creativity and Natural Language Generation, pages 5–10,
Tilburg, November 2018.

the characteristics of a text for it to be considered a narrative. It also helps the study of specific storytelling strategies to foster emotional responses of the reader which helps to measure the degree of interestingness of the text.

Herman's work on the basic elements of narrative presents us four main elements divided into: (1) situatednes, (2) event sequencing, (3) world making/ world disruption and (4) what it's like. What makes his approach to stand out is the focus given on the fourth element: for him, narratives are stories about things that happened to particular people and what it was like for the to experience that. Thus, he uses Monika Fludernik's concept of experientiality in which narrativity is based on the evocation of a human-like consciousness (Herman, 2013).

So, the main focus of this approach is to perceive the strategies used in narratives to affect the reader somehow, through triggering unconscious feelings. Another aspect of this approach is the exploration of characters and characterization techniques, especially the ones that deal with the relationships among the characters.

As the approach does not discard formalization, it helps to understand or even develop a model of narrative worldmaking using: who, what, when, where, how, why (Herman, 2013). It is worth highlighting that all these analyses take into consideration all the social and cultural aspects of the texts.

The search for a new approach in Narratology is to propose the experimentation of the language using a more contemporary and natural model of narrative (Fludernik, 1996).

6 Literary Corpora

Because most narrative generation systems are in the realm of the fantastic or fairy tales, this work proposes the experimentation with a different kind of narrative text. To try a more natural approach with a more social appeal, the urban novel was the choice for an ontology because they tend to observe people and understand/ describe social relations in the urban environment. This kind of novel has a direct correspondence between text and reality. It is realist not because it represents real life, but because of the way reality is represented through a great variety of human experiences.

Although Brazilian Romantic Urban Novel is not such a breakthrough in terms of literary genre,

WHO	WHAT
The mistress	Stays with married man
The single strong woman	Reads, discusses politics, empowers other women
The wife	Stays home, suffers, conspires against mistress
The rich single man	Tries to get strong woman
The romantic single man	Tries to get strong woman
The husband	Works, goes to bar, goes to brothel
The priest/ Family members	Interfere in the other characters choices

Table 1: Characters (Who) & Action (What)

WHERE	WHEN
Street/Bar/Brothel	The married man is at the brothel/ street
Street/Café/Home	Whenever she is provoked
Home/Church	Most of the time
Street/ Work/ Bar/ Brothel	Whenever he feels like
Street/ Home/ Bar/ Café	Whenever he meets woman
Street/ Home/ work	When he needs to feel powerful
Church/ Home	Most of the time

Table 2: Place (Where) & Time (When)

it serves our purposes to try to develop a different narrative model for a prototype of a narrative generator once it presents a fixed structure and a certain number of characters. The plot is also well organized in terms of time and space. There is a large number of texts available in public domain.

Mainly focused on the female audience from the beginning of Brazilian modernization, by the end of the 19th century, these novels presented fixed structures and simple language. Most of the plots were steady – even when they presented different sub-plots that merged. The characters used to depict social groups and could be less complex than the characters of the following literary schools. Love is the main motif and it is always related to the social values of the time. They are usually (impossible) love stories told with some humor in a linear time and space.

The following tables show a first attempt to obtain a general model of the Brazilian Urban Novel through the personal analysis of the following books: A Moreninha (Macedo, 1844), Senhora (Alencar, 1875), Diva (Alencar, 1864), Lucíola (Alencar, 1862). The model was based on Herman's Basic Elements of Narative (2009).

7 Final Remarks

The main objective of this paper was not to find answers but mainly raise questions to be further

Proceedings of the 3rd Workshop on Computational Creativity and Natural Language Generation, pages 5–10,
Tilburg, November 2018. ©2018 Association for Computational Linguistics

HOW	WHY
Destroying the man's marriage	Wants money/ wants better life
Arguing with men/ helping other women	Wants to be free from society
With the help of strong woman or rich man	Wants revenge
Flirting with strong woman	Wants to get strong woman
Flirting with strong woman	Wants to marry strong woman
Staying with mistress/ fighting rich man	Wants revenge from rich man
Giving their opinion/ confounding the characters	No main objective

Table 3: Plot (How) & Objective (Why)

answered throughout the development of the research.

At this point, the study of Cognitive Narratology applied to the generation of narrative seems to be a good path for the development of systems more cognitive-social oriented. Compared to the previous approaches, it helps us to understand narratives as human experiences and try to replicate it in order to improve the interestingness of the output focusing on affecting the reader.

Even if this approach cannot be used to develop a system from scratch, it would be helpful to be applied in existing systems to test its applicability, even though it is still a first draft of the model.

Since urban novels are very distinct from folktales it is necessary to observe its own characteristics and find the paradigms to formalize this kind of text. At this point, some particularities were already found as showed in the tables.The next step would be the formalization of the narrative genre – work in progress – to be further tested in the prototype.

References

José Alencar. 1862. *Lucíola*. Public Domain.

José Alencar. 1864. *Diva*. Public Domain.

José Alencar. 1875. *Senhora*. Public Domain.

Selmer Bringsjord and David Ferrucci. 1999. *Artificial Intelligence and Literary Creativity: Inside the Mind of BRUTUS, a Storytelling Machine*. Lawrence Erlbaum Associates, Hillsdale, NJ.

Monika Fludernik. 1996. *Towards a 'natural' narratology*, volume 25. Routledge, NY.

Hugo Goncalo Oliveira. 2017. A Survey on Intelligent Poetry Generation: Languages, Features, Techniques, Reutilisation and Evaluation. *Proceedings of The 10th International Natural Language Generation conference (INLG'17)*, pages 11–20.

David Herman. 2000. Narratology as a cognitive science. *Image & Narrative*, 1(1):1–26.

David Herman. 2009. *Basic Elements of Narrative*. Blackwell Publishing, Malden, MA.

David Herman. 2013. Cognitive Narratology.

Shohei Imabuchi and Takashi Ogata. 2014. Integrating the Event Generation Mechanism in the Propp-based Story Generation Mechanism into the Integrated Narrative Generation System. *Journal of Robotics, Networking and Aritficial Life*, 1(2):164–168.

Ben Kybartas and Rafael Bidarra. 2017. A Survey on Story Generation Techniques for Authoring Computational Narratives. *IEEE Transactions on Computational Intelligence and AI in Games*, 9(3):239–253.

George Lakoff. 1972. Structural complexity in fairy tales. *The Study of man ; v. 1.*, 1:. 128–150.

Claude Lévi-Strauss. 1955. The Structural Study fo Myth. *The Journal of American Folklore*, 68(270):428–444.

Joaquim Manuel de Macedo. 1844. *A Moreninha*. 91. Public Domain.

Federico Peinado and Pablo Gervás. 2005. Creativity issues in plot generation. In *Workshop on Computational Creativity, Working Notes. 19th International Joint Conference on Artificial Intelligence*, International Joint Conference on Artificial Intelligence 2005, Edinburgh, Scotland. School of Informatics, University of Edinburgh, School of Informatics, University of Edinburgh.

Lyn Pemberton. 1984. *Story Structure: A Narrative Grammar of Nine Chansons de Geste of the Guillaume d'Orange Cycle*. Ph.D. thesis, University of Toronto.

Lyn Pemberton. 1989. A modular approach to story generation. *Proceedings of the fourth conference on European* {...}, pages 217–224.

Rafael Pérez y Pérez. 1999. *MEXICA : A Computer Model of Creativity in Writing*. Ph.D. thesis, University of Sussex.

Rafael Pérez y Pérez. 2018. The Computational Creativity Continuum. In *Proceedings of the Ninth International Conference on Computational Creativity ICCC 2018*, pages 177–184.

Vladímir Propp. 1968. *Morphology of the Folktale (Translated by The American Folklore Society and Indiana University)*. Bloomington, Indiana University.

Proceedings of the 3rd Workshop on Computational Creativity and Natural Language Generation, pages 5–10,
Tilburg, November 2018. ©2018 Association for Computational Linguistics

Mark O Riedl. 2004. *Narrative Planning: Balancing Plot and Character.* Ph.D. thesis, North Carolina University.

Brandon Tearse, Noah Wardrip-fruin, and Michael Mateas. 2010. Minstrel Remixed : Procedurally Generating Stories. *Artificial Intelligence*, pages 192–197.

Tzvetan Todorov. 1975. *The Fantastic: A Structural Approach to a Literary Genre*, 1st edition. Cornell University Press.

Scott R Turner. 1993. *MINSTREL: A computer model of creativity and storytelling.* Ph.d., University of California.

Proceedings of the 3rd Workshop on Computational Creativity and Natural Language Generation, pages 5–10,
Tilburg, November 2018.

Discourse Embellishment Using a Deep Encoder-Decoder Network

Leonid Berov
Institute of Cognitive Science
University of Osnabrück, Germany
lberov@uos.de

Kai Standvoss
Donders Institute for Brain, Cognition and Behaviour
Radboud University, The Netherlands
kstandvoss@uos.de

Abstract

We suggest a new NLG task in the context of the discourse generation pipeline of computational storytelling systems. This task, textual embellishment, is defined by taking a text as input and generating a semantically equivalent output with increased lexical and syntactic complexity. Ideally, this would allow the authors of computational storytellers to implement just lightweight NLG systems and use a domain-independent embellishment module to translate its output into more literary text. We present promising first results on this task using LSTM Encoder-Decoder networks trained on the WikiLarge dataset. Furthermore, we introduce "Compiled Computer Tales", a corpus of computationally generated stories, that can be used to test the capabilities of embellishment algorithms.

1 Introduction

Narratives can be analyzed to consist of at least two layers: plot—what is told—and discourse—how it is told. Usually, computational systems first generate the events of the plot, and then decide how to render these in text (Gervás, 2009). This means that a tight coupling exists between the knowledge bases that are used for plot generation, and the NLG modules for discourse rendering. The result is that it is hard to share these modules between systems, while the implementation of a custom module to generate literary discourse requires significant effort and linguistic expertise. Indeed, our subjective feeling is that often it is possible to recognize repeating textual patterns when reading several stories created by the same system.

To alleviate this problems we suggest a new NLG task, *textual embellishment* (TE), with the goal to automatically increase the lexical and syntactic complexity of a text. Textual embellishment can be understood as the inverse task to textual simplification (TS), which has been researched for at least two decades (Shardlow, 2014). Recent TS systems are trained on vast corpora using machine learning techniques and work independent of domains or handcrafted rules. These results open the intriguing possibility for an equally general resource for TE. This could allow the authors of storytelling systems to safe time by implementing only thin NLG modules and perform subsequent embellishment. We would like to strongly caution that TE most likely will prove to be a more difficult task then TS. While the latter typically results in removing information in a text, the former might lead to an automated adding of information which can introduce semantic contradictions. However, on a syntactic level TE ideally just results in periphrastic constructions with no added information.

2 Related Work

Traditionally, narrative generation systems like Meehan (1977); Lebowitz (1985) were devised to generate macro-level plot and character elements without connecting them into a comprehensive story in natural language. Later work has sought to combine plot and NLG into a unified system (Callaway and Lester, 2002). These full pipelines generate story elements and employ rule-based language models that produce naturally sounding narratives. While these approaches make use of text embellishment, the disadvantage of these rule-based approaches is that rules for text enrichment have to be conceived of in advance by the system's architect. The work presented here, in contrast, seeks to learn a natural language representation

Proceedings of the 3rd Workshop on Computational Creativity and Natural Language Generation, pages 11–16,
Tilburg, November 2018. ©2018 Association for Computational Linguistics

from human data to automatically embellish priorly generated narratives.

This approach can be located in the field of natural language processing. Within this area of research several related subfields can be identified, including text summarisation, statistical machine translation, and most notably, TS. Both, text summarisation and simplification, seek to extract the relevant information of a phrase and lose all linguistic embellishment that is deemed unnecessary for its understanding. Our work has a complementary objective, which is enriching text while maintaining its original meaning. This generative task is related to recent developments in computer vision using Generative Adversarial Networks for problems like image super resolution (Ledig et al., 2017). Therein similar challenges are faced as new information has to be "hallucinated", requiring particular caution in content sensitive domains.

Within TS, Shardlow (2014) distinguishes between syntactic and lexical simplification. While the former approach seeks to facilitate readability by reducing the complexity of sentence structure, the latter seeks to replace words deemed difficult for a target audience by words that are easier understandable. Previous work has focused on both tasks individually (Siddharthan, 2006; Paetzold and Specia, 2017), while recent approaches addressed syntactic and lexical simplification simultaneously (Wang et al., 2016; Zhang and Lapata, 2017). These latter systems cast text simplification as a monolingual machine translation problem and borrow insights from automatic natural language generation (Wen et al., 2015). Therein, the task of simplifying text is framed as a translation problem between "complex English" and "simple English". The recent success of Deep Learning systems in "neural machine translation" (Bahdanau et al., 2014; Cho et al., 2014) has increased the employment, specifically of the LSTM encoder-decoder architecture (Sutskever et al., 2014). These models make use of the Long Short-Term Memory neural network architecture (Hochreiter and Schmidhuber, 1997) to solve a sequence to sequence task. Therein, a mapping from a *source* sequence to a *target* sequence is learned both of which may be of variable length . To that goal, an *encoder* LSTM generates a sequence of hidden representations using the source, which is then used by a second *decoder* LSTM to generate the target sequence word by word, whereof each is conditioned on all previous outputs. Here, we follow the same approach but address the opposite problem to TS, translating from "simple" to "complex" English, building on the success of previous neural network approaches.

3 Discourse Embellishment

For the trained network, two LSTM layers per encoder and decoder were chosen, since Wang et al. (2016) demonstrated that this is sufficient for sorting, reversing and reordering operations in a textual simplification task. The network was set up and trained using Harvard's OpenNMT-tf framework (Klein et al., 2017). Parameters were selected as suggested by Zhang and Lapata (2017): Each layer contained 512 hidden units with weights uniformly initialized to [-0.1, 0.1], learning was performed with a 0.2 dropout rate (Zaremba et al., 2014) and Luong attention was used by the decoder (Luong et al., 2015). If not stated otherwise, training was always performed for 24 epochs, with a learning rate of 1 and a simple gradient descent optimization, where gradients where clipped when their norm exceeded 5 (Pascanu et al., 2013). After 18 epochs a decay rate of 0.25 was applied each epoch. Furthermore, pre-trained 300 dimensional GloVe vectors were used to initialize word embeddings (Pennington et al., 2014), and the vocabulary size was 50,000.

3.1 Story Corpus

The performance of a discourse embellishment system should ideally be judged on domain-specific texts. To the best of our knowledge no corpus of computationally generated stories has been compiled so far. Since no common resources for NLG generation have been deployed, the stories that have been generated by different systems over the decades differ markedly in their language.

To reflect this diversity we decided for a breadth-focused approach while setting up *Compiled Computer Tales* (CCT), a corpus of computationally generated stories. Since the aim of this corpus is to be used as a qualitative test set, and not as training data for machine learning algorithms, we collected at most three stories from as many systems as available to us, instead of compiling many stories from few systems. Because it is unfeasible to deploy all individual systems, we instead opted for using stories that have been reported in scientific publications, although this runs

Proceedings of the 3rd Workshop on Computational Creativity and Natural Language Generation, pages 11–16,
Tilburg, November 2018. ©2018 Association for Computational Linguistics

the danger of biasing the corpus towards high-quality exemplars.[1] The resulting corpus can be found online[2] and we cordially invite researchers to expand this necessarily incomplete collection.

At the moment of writing, it contains 14 stories from 8 storytellers, ranging from early systems like "Novel Writer" (Klein et al., 1973) to recent ones like "Simlextric" (Riegl and Veale, 2018). It is formatted in a way that allows separation based on system, story, paragraph (45 in total) or sentence (290 in total); depending on the task at hand. We also provide a python script that can be used to perform such splits, as well as common pre-processing steps like tokenization or named entity anonymization.

3.2 Sentence Based: Lexical Embellishment

As with the more common TS task, we trained our network on a sentence-aligned dataset. The largest simplification dataset is, to the best of our knowledge, WikiLarge, which contains 296,402 automatically aligned sentences from the ordinary and simple English Wikipedias in its training set. To reduce vocabulary, named entities in the dataset were anonymized (Zhang and Lapata, 2017).

Unlike for simplification, for the present task the network was trained to generate original ('complex') English based on simple English input. The performance of the system is evaluated using the common BLEU metric (Papineni et al., 2002), which measures the degree to which generated embellished text differs from the language employed in the original Wikipedia. Training is continuously evaluated on a held-out evaluation set using the Moses toolkit (Koehn et al., 2007), and BLEU stagnates after around 18 epochs. The final performance on the held-out test set is a BLEU of 56.02 on the tokenized data, which is a reasonable performance[3].

To judge the performance of this model on CCT, the corpus had to be split in sentences, tokenized, and named entities had to be anonymized in a manner comparable to WikiLarge. Since no gold-standard of embellished tales exists, quantitative evaluation of embellishment quality is not possible. Comparing the embellished version with the original ones shows that the network mostly learned to correctly reproduce its input (BLEU 92.13). If differences that are due only to out-of-vocabulary words and minor formatting differences are ignored, then roughly 83% of the sentences are simply reproductions of the input. Around 5% of the generated sentences do not bear any resemblance to the corresponding input, which we consider to happen when the network overfitted a certain type of input. 2% of the generated sentences miss individual words. The remaining 10% contain syntactically correct lexical substitutions, which can be considered cases of lexical embellishment. Some examples of felicitous embellishment are the mappings: *Because of this* → *consequently* ‖ *tried* → *attempted* ‖ *wanted to* → *sought to* ‖ *bossy* → *overbearing*; while examples of failed embellishment are: *sinful* → *drinking* ‖ *lioness* → *cat* ‖ *ubiquitous* → *familiar* ‖ *towards princess* → *towards LOCATION@1*.

3.3 Paragraph Based: Degradation

Sentence aligned training enabled the network to perform lexical embellishment, however, no syntactical embellishment like concatenation or parenthetical insertion was observed. It stands to reason that such sentence-level reordering can be better picked up by learning from a corpus that aligns whole paragraphs, where several sentence are simplified/embellished at a time. A promising candidate is the document aligned Wikipedia corpus compiled by Kauchak (2013). After the necessary preprocessing and splitting steps the resulting dataset contained 134,233 paragraphs in the training set.

Training a network on this dataset using the same setup was not successful. The model achieved a BLEU score of 3.55 on the held-out test set, which is a clear sign of its failure.

A manual inspection of the dataset revealed, that the employed alignment of paragraphs is rarely meaningful, since paragraphs of the same ordinal number often fail to contain semantically related information, let alone simplified/embellished versions of each other. In fact, further literature review did not reveal work on either paragraph or document aligned simplification, as well as no published results using the document

[1] A notable exception is "Simlextric" (Riegl and Veale, 2018), which is accessible online and was used to generate novel stories for the corpus.

[2] https://github.com/cartisan/CompiledComputerTales

[3] The state of the art system from 2014 achieves a worse BLEU of 48.97 on the considerably easier textual simplification task using this dataset. However, current state of the art strongly outperforms this with a BLEU of 88.85, again, on the simpler text simplification task (Zhang and Lapata, 2017).

Proceedings of the 3rd Workshop on Computational Creativity and Natural Language Generation, pages 11–16,
Tilburg, November 2018.

aligned dataset. This lead us to suspect that the encountered problems are not of trivial nature, and abandon this direction of inquiry.

3.4 Pair Based: Syntactical Embellishment

An inspection of the WikiLarge dataset revealed that the sought-for syntactical reorderings can also be found there. In particular, the sentence-alignment does not necessarily result in a bijective mapping from complex to simple sentences, but sometimes in a 1:2 mapping, when complex sentences are split in two. This lead us to the hypothesis that the network described in section 3.2 should already be able to perform syntactical embellishment, when presented with two input sentences.

To test this we pre-processed the CCT corpus by concatenating, with a space, two consecutive sentences. This resulted in sentence-pairs that in most cases had the potential to be combined, because they shared subjects or were causally related. In some cases, syntactical combinations were not meaningful, especially when sentence pairs crossed paragraph or story boundaries as a result of the unsophisticated concatenation operation.

Comparing the embellished version with the original ones shows that the network is doing an acceptable job in keeping original and embellishment related (BLEU 68.20). Approximately 56% of the generated pairs were combined by the network into one sentence. In 42% of the cases the network did not combine the pairs, in which case it usually kept the first sentence and removed the second. In the remaining 2% the networks output was not related to the input.

The combination of sentences was performed by the network in different ways. Most commonly, it conjoined them using a comma and the conjunction *and*, or replaced the period sign with a comma, while changing the following letter to lower case. We also observed cases where the pronouns *who, which* or *where* were employed. Another mode of combining sentences employed by the network was by using participles: *...she robbed PERSON@2 of her illusions . She said : " PERSON@3 took ... "* $\rightarrow$ *...she robbed PERSON@2 of her illusions* **, saying** *: " PERSON@3 took ... "*. The most interesting case appeared to involve an inclusion: *PERSON@1 saw the affair . PERSON@1 was jealous* $\rightarrow$ *PERSON@1* ***was jealous of*** *the affair*. In a previous run the same sentence was embellished using nominalisation: *PERSON@1 saw the affair* ***with jealousy***. For more context, a comparison between an original and a pair-embellished story can be found in the appendix.

4 Conclusion

NLG systems in computational storytellers are commonly dependent on the systems' knowledge base and require idiosyncratic, hand-coded rules if complex language output is desired. Based on this observation we propose to extend the discourse generation pipeline with a TE step that takes as input simple English sentences and performs a monolingual translation into lexically and syntactically more complex English. This approach has the benefit of allowing the authors of storytellers to save time by implementing only simple custom text generation modules, and employ a domain-independent embellishment module to translate into more sophisticated text.

The LSTM Encoder-Decoder approach explored in this paper is not ready for productive use as is, mainly because it does not always fail gracefully, i.e. produces well-formed and semantically appropriate language when embellishment fails. However, it shows promising results by demonstrating that the same trained network is capable of producing interesting lexical as well as syntactical embellishment of varying kind.

We are confident that the presented results can be improved by employing techniques that have proven beneficial in a simplification setting, like e.g. the reinforcement learning proposed by Zhang and Lapata (2017). Due to the nature of the corpus we used for training, only those entries could contribute to the performance of syntactical embellishment that contained two sentences on the simple English, and one on the normal English side. At the same time, the language employed in the Wikipedia can be expected to be markedly different from the one usually aimed for by storytelling systems, which has an impact on lexical embellishment performance. Hence, further improvements can be expected from using more—or better suited—corpora, like e.g. Newsela (Xu et al., 2015). Another promising option would be to explore the viability of embellishment/simplification datasets based on an alignment of simple English versions of novels with their original counterparts. To exceed sentence-

Proceedings of the 3rd Workshop on Computational Creativity and Natural Language Generation, pages 11–16,
Tilburg, November 2018. ©2018 Association for Computational Linguistics

pair based processing, paragraph aligned versions of text would prove to be valuable resources.

Apart from the above theoretical and technological contributions we also presented a first version of Compiled Computer Tales, a corpus of computer generated stories. This corpus can be used to test the capabilities of embellishment algorithms, as well as for historiographic inquiries. We cordially invite collaboration to complete its coverage.

Acknowledgment

The first author is grateful for a Humboldt PhD fellowship.

References

Dzmitry Bahdanau, Kyunghyun Cho, and Yoshua Bengio. 2014. Neural machine translation by jointly learning to align and translate. *arXiv preprint arXiv:1409.0473*.

Charles B. Callaway and James C. Lester. 2002. Narrative prose generation. *Artif. Intell.*, 139(2):213–252.

Kyunghyun Cho, Bart Van Merriënboer, Caglar Gulcehre, Dzmitry Bahdanau, Fethi Bougares, Holger Schwenk, and Yoshua Bengio. 2014. Learning phrase representations using rnn encoder-decoder for statistical machine translation. *arXiv preprint arXiv:1406.1078*.

Pablo Gervás. 2009. Computational approaches to storytelling and creativity. *AI Magazine*, 30(3):49–62.

Sepp Hochreiter and Jürgen Schmidhuber. 1997. Long short-term memory. *Neural computation*, 9(8):1735–1780.

David Kauchak. 2013. Improving text simplification language modeling using unsimplified text data. In *Proceedings of the 51st ACL*, volume 1, pages 1537–1546.

Guillaume Klein, Yoon Kim, Yuntian Deng, Jean Senellart, and Alexander M. Rush. 2017. OpenNMT: Open-source toolkit for neural machine translation. *arXiv preprint arXiv:1701.02810*.

Sheldon Klein, J. Aeschlimann, and D. Balsiger. 1973. Automatic novel writing: A status report. *Technical Report 186, Computer Science Department, The University of Wisconsin, Madison, Wisconsin.*

Philipp Koehn, Hieu Hoang, Alexandra Birch, Chris Callison-Burch, Marcello Federico, Nicola Bertoldi, Brooke Cowan, Wade Shen, Christine Moran, and Richard Zens. 2007. MOSES: Open source toolkit for statistical machine translation. In *Proceedings of the 45th ACL*, pages 177–180. Association for Computational Linguistics.

Michael Lebowitz. 1985. Story-telling as planning and learning. *Poetics*, 14(6):483–502.

Christian Ledig, Lucas Theis, Ferenc Huszár, Jose Caballero, Andrew Cunningham, Alejandro Acosta, Andrew P Aitken, Alykhan Tejani, Johannes Totz, Zehan Wang, et al. 2017. Photo-realistic single image super-resolution using a generative adversarial network. In *CVPR*, volume 2, page 4.

Minh-Thang Luong, Hieu Pham, and Christopher D. Manning. 2015. Effective approaches to attention-based neural machine translation. *arXiv preprint arXiv:1508.04025*.

James R Meehan. 1977. Tale-spin, an interactive program that writes stories. In *IJCAI*, volume 77, pages 91–98.

Gustavo H. Paetzold and Lucia Specia. 2017. A survey on lexical simplification. *JAIR*, 60:549–593.

Kishore Papineni, Salim Roukos, Todd Ward, and Wei-Jing Zhu. 2002. BLEU: a method for automatic evaluation of machine translation. In *Proceedings of the 40th ACL*, pages 311–318. Association for Computational Linguistics.

Razvan Pascanu, Tomas Mikolov, and Yoshua Bengio. 2013. On the difficulty of training recurrent neural networks. In *Proceedings of the 30th ICML*, pages 1310–1318.

Jeffrey Pennington, Richard Socher, and Christopher Manning. 2014. GloVe: Global vectors for word representation. In *Proceedings of the 19th EMNLP*, pages 1532–1543.

Stefan Riegl and Tony Veale. 2018. Live, die, evaluate, repeat: Do-over simulation in the generation of coherent episodic stories. In *Proceedings of the 9th ICCC*, pages 80–87, Salamanca, Spain. Association for Computational Creativity.

Matthew Shardlow. 2014. A survey of automated text simplification. *IJACSA*, 4(1):58–70.

Advaith Siddharthan. 2006. Syntactic simplification and text cohesion. *Res. Lang. Comput.*, 4(1):77–109.

Ilya Sutskever, Oriol Vinyals, and Quoc V. Le. 2014. Sequence to sequence learning with neural networks. In *Adv Neural Inform Process Syst*, pages 3104–3112.

Tong Wang, Ping Chen, Kevin Amaral, and Jipeng Qiang. 2016. An experimental study of LSTM encoder-decoder model for text simplification. *arXiv preprint arXiv:1609.03663*.

Tsung-Hsien Wen, Milica Gasic, Nikola Mrksic, Pei-Hao Su, David Vandyke, and Steve Young. 2015. Semantically conditioned LSTM-based natural language generation for spoken dialogue systems. *arXiv preprint arXiv:1508.01745*.

Proceedings of the 3rd Workshop on Computational Creativity and Natural Language Generation, pages 11–16,
Tilburg, November 2018. ©2018 Association for Computational Linguistics

Wei Xu, Chris Callison-Burch, and Courtney Napoles. 2015. Problems in current text simplification research: New data can help. *TACL*, 3(1):283–297.

Wojciech Zaremba, Ilya Sutskever, and Oriol Vinyals. 2014. Recurrent neural network regularization. *arXiv preprint arXiv:1409.2329*.

Xingxing Zhang and Mirella Lapata. 2017. Sentence simplification with deep reinforcement learning. In *Proceedings of the 22nd EMNLP*, pages 584–594, Copenhagen, Denmark.

Appendix

Original (Riegl and Veale, 2018) and embellished stories, using the pair-based method:

PERSON@1 needed a place to live and PERSON@2 had plenty of it . PERSON@1 found PERSON@2 at an underground lair . PERSON@1 rented accommodation from her . She paid PERSON@2 what she owed . LOCATION@1 could not achieve bossy PERSON@1 's lofty goals . She refused to honour PERSON@2 's commitments to her , so PERSON@1 ripped off rich PERSON@2 's best ideas . PERSON@1 PERSON@2 evicted PERSON@3 from LOCATION@1 's home . At a smoke-filled back room PERSON@3 met PERSON@4 . LOCATION@1 assiduously curried favor with dictatorial Oscar after cheated PERSON@1 evicted PERSON@2 from LOCATION@2 's home . PERSON@2 told eager Wilde a pack of lies . PERSON@1 said : " Dolores wrote propaganda to promote your cause . " His attitude hardened toward LOCATION@1 . He openly disrespected PERSON@1 because earlier she took everything that PERSON@2 had . PERSON@1 tried to tune out loudmouthed PERSON@3 's voice . LOCATION@1 PERSON@1 wrote PERSON@2 off as a loser , so he coldly dismissed PERSON@2 and turned away . It was at the red carpet when PERSON@2 found LOCATION@2 . PERSON@1 started a new job for influential Rina after unsatisfied PERSON@2 told PERSON@1 to get out and not come back . PERSON@3 took full advantage of her . She pulled the wool over PERSON@1 's eyes . She said : " PERSON@2 was a real suck-up to aristocratic PERSON@3 . " LOCATION@1 could not reach the bar set by bossy LOCATION@2 . She was very disappointed in her , so " Get out ! You 're fired " said PERSON@1 . It was at a recording studio when PERSON@2 found PERSON@3 . LOCATION@1 PERSON@1 recruited PERSON@2 into her ranks after PERSON@3 asked her to clear out her desk and leave . PERSON@2 took the spotlight from lackadaisical Dolores . PERSON@1 withheld due payment from lazy Maura . PERSON@2 criticized sinful Dolores in public . She said : " PERSON@1 showed no shame in sucking up to influential PERSON@2 . " She broke with her and went her own way . What do you think ? Can PERSON@1 and PERSON@2 ever mend their relationship ?

PERSON@1 needed a place to live and PERSON@2 had plenty of it , and PERSON@1 found PERSON@2 at an underground lair . PERSON@1 rented accommodation from her and paid PERSON@2 what she owed . LOCATION@1 could not achieve overbearing PERSON@1 's lofty goals and refused to honor PERSON@2 's commitments to her , so PERSON@1 ripped off rich PERSON@2 's best ideas . PERSON@1 PERSON@2 evicted from LOCATION@1 's home , and at a smoke-filled back room PERSON@3 met PERSON@4 . LOCATION@1 assiduously curried favor with dictatorial Oscar after cheated PERSON@1 evicted PERSON@2 from LOCATION@2 's home , who told eager a pack of lies . PERSON@1 said : " Dolores wrote propaganda to promote your cause " . He openly disrespected PERSON@1 because earlier she took everything that PERSON@2 had , and PERSON@1 tried to tune out loudmouthed PERSON@3 's voice . LOCATION@1 PERSON@1 wrote PERSON@2 off as a loser , so he coldly dismissed PERSON@2 and turned away at the red carpet when PERSON@2 found LOCATION@2 . PERSON@1 started a new job for influential Rina after unsatisfied PERSON@2 told PERSON@1 to get out and not come back . She pulled the wool over PERSON@1 's eyes , saying : " PERSON@2 was a real suck-up to aristocratic PERSON@3 . " LOCATION@1 could not reach the bar set by overbearing LOCATION@2 , and she was very disappointed in her , so " Get out ! You 're fired " said PERSON@1 , at a recording studio when PERSON@2 discovered PERSON@3 . LOCATION@1 PERSON@1 recruited PERSON@2 into her ranks after PERSON@3 asked her to clear out her desk and leave . PERSON@1 withheld due payment from lazy Maura . She said : " PERSON@1 exhibited no shame in digestion up to influential PERSON@2 " she broke with her and went her own way . What do you think ?

Proceedings of the 3rd Workshop on Computational Creativity and Natural Language Generation, pages 11–16, Tilburg, November 2018. ©2018 Association for Computational Linguistics

Exploring Lexical-Semantic Knowledge in the Generation of Novel Riddles in Portuguese

Hugo Gonçalo Oliveira
CISUC, DEI
University of Coimbra, Portugal
hroliv@dei.uc.pt

Ricardo Rodrigues
CISUC
Polytechnic Institute of Coimbra, Portugal
rmanuel@dei.uc.pt

Abstract

We describe an effort towards the automatic generation of novel riddles in Portuguese, ultimately with humour value. Riddle generation fits in the common architecture of a NLG system and may follow different models, described here, all based on features of a concept, acquired from a lexical-semantic knowledge base. Generated riddles were manually assessed by humans, who rated them as fairly interpretable, surprising, and novel, even if with low humour potential.

1 Introduction

To act naturally, computers should be able to entertain, e.g., with the creation of wordplay or humour. This paper is about the automatic generation of novel riddles, which would ideally be apt for humorous contexts. Riddles are a kind of linguistic puzzle, present in most cultures and languages. They can be posed as a question, followed by a short hiatus — allowing for the audience to think —, and finally an answer that works as a punchline. Their generation is closely related to the topic of Computational Humour (Ritchie et al., 2006), which studies the utilisation of humour by computers, with value for Natural Language Understanding — specifically, developing models for automatically recognising and understanding humour (Mihalcea and Strapparava, 2006; Yang et al., 2015) —, and for Natural Language Generation (NLG) — developing systems that produce verbal humour (see section 2), which is our case.

Both riddles and humour have been generated by others, following different approaches, but often in English. Our work is inspired by the previous and represents an effort towards the development of a riddle generator in Portuguese. We exploit available lexical resources for this language, mainly a semantic knowledge base, and implement six models for generating novel riddles, hopefully funny, due to the introduction of potentially incongruent word-play, forcing the re-interpretation of known concepts or the creation of new ones. This is a follow-up, as we have previously proposed the six generation models in a single-page paper (Gonçalo Oliveira and Rodrigues, 2018) and analysed the results of different word sources, relations, presentation modes, and automatic scoring, for two of those models (Gonçalo Oliveira and Rodrigues, 2018b).

We frame our current results as *piadas secas* (roughly, dry jokes) which, in Portugal, are a kind of joke that may be presented as a riddle, with a question and a short not-so-funny, obvious or nonsensical answer, taking advantage of the anti-climax to make people laugh. In 2017, this kind of jokes seemed to have had a comeback, as they were used in several television shows and YouTube videos, and re-compiled in websites or edited books (Pinto et al., 2017). This is why the system is baptised as SECO (dry).

The remainder of the paper starts with a brief overview on related work, covering the generation of riddles and verbal humour. The steps for the generation of riddles with the help of a knowledge base are then described, with some examples. Before concluding, we present the results of human validation of generated riddles, illustrated with additional examples. According to human subjects, riddles are accessible, surprising and novel, but, on average, not so funny.

2 Related Work

Riddles have long been a research topic. Georges and Dundes (1963) define them as "*a traditional verbal expression which contains one or more descriptive elements, a pair of which may be in opposition; the referent of the elements is to be guessed*." Palma and Weiner (1992) confirm that lexical ambiguity, arising, for instance, from pol-

Proceedings of the 3rd Workshop on Computational Creativity and Natural Language Generation, pages 17–25,
Tilburg, November 2018.

ysemy or homophony, is paramount to their creation, alongside the association of words to *ad-hoc* categories, according to their multiple meanings.

Riddle generation by computer programs has been addressed in the 1990s, with the seminal work of Binsted and Ritchie (1994), who developed JAPE, a system that generates punning riddles based on a syntactic and semantic lexicon; a set of schemata for combining two words based on their lexical or phonetic relationship; and a set of templates that render riddles as text. An example of a riddle would be "*What do you call a murderer that has fibre? A cereal killer.*" STANDUP (Manurung et al., 2008) adopts a similar approach, but is more cautious on the words used, restricted at various levels for a better output and suitability for the intended audiences.

TheRiddlerBot (Guerrero et al., 2015) generates riddles about famous characters. After selecting a well-known name from a knowledge base: associated features are retrieved; analogous characters, with common features, are identified; a textual template is selected for rendering the riddle, based on some of the features or the analogy; the riddle is posted in Twitter; and aliases are retrieved from Wikipedia, so that users may answer with the name of the selected character or one of its aliases. An example of a riddle for the Joker would be: "*Tell me the name of a person that is the Morpheus of The Dark Knight Rises, is criminal, playful yet cruel, has been seen wearing a purple topcoat.*"

Riddles have also been generated from word associations (Galvan et al., 2016). Given a concept: its possible categories are obtained from a creative thesaurus; associated modifiers are also retrieved and one is randomly selected; new categories, to which the selected modifier is associated to, are retrieved; a final category is composed by combining the selected modifier with one of the new categories; a concept of the final category is used to fill a text template. An example of a riddle for the sun would be "*What is as hot as soup?*" Unlike JAPE and STANDUP, this system and TheRiddlerBot do not tackle the humour aspect specifically.

The ConceptNet semantic network was exploited for the generation of verbal humour, including riddles (Labutov and Lipson, 2012). For this purpose, different, but overlapping, paths between the same two concepts are aligned with a surface template that maximises inter-path incongruity. For question-answer riddles, the question mentions two concepts from different paths, but same domain, while the concept in the answer is in one of the paths, but from a different domain. An example of a riddle is "*Why is the computer in hospital? Because the computer has virus.*"

Besides riddles, there is work on the generation of other kinds of verbal humour, including funny acronyms (Stock and Strapparava, 2006), or short messages (Valitutti et al., 2016). Both explore lexical replacement for potentiating humour. Replacement words are constrained by the original form (same initial letter or similar sound) and possibly other humour-specific features (e.g., taboo).

All of the previous works generate riddles or humour based on some theory and knowledge resources, essential for their goal. They share a number of similarities with ours, but they all produce text in English. A few exceptions generate humour in other languages (e.g., Sjöbergh and Araki (2007)), but none generates riddles in Portuguese. In this language, however, there is work on the automatic generation of Internet humour (Gonçalo Oliveira et al., 2016), based on an image macro and a line of text.

Humour occurs when there is a break of conventionality in language. Understanding it is a sign of fluency (Tagnin, 2005), which explains the interest of computational linguistics on this topic. Humour is generally based on four linguistic phenomena, at the written and oral levels (Tagnin, 2005), namely: homonymy — words with the same spelling and sound, e.g., 'band', musical group or ring —, homophony — words with the same sound, but different spellings, e.g., cent and scent —, polysemy — words with the same spelling and sound, but multiple related meanings, e.g., wood, timber or forest —, and paronymy — words with similar spellings or sounds, e.g., collision and collusion. As such, its success depends highly on how proficient the audience is in the language used.

According to Attardo (2008), humorous plots can rely on one of the following: a punch line (typical jokes); a meta-narrative disruption, introducing familiar humorous references; or an otherwise normal situation, where some elements may cause laughter by the shortcomings of the agents.

3 Riddle Generation Approach

SECO explores lexical resources in Portuguese for generating word and feature combinations. Those can be rendered as novel riddles, to be used for

Proceedings of the 3rd Workshop on Computational Creativity and Natural Language Generation, pages 17–25,
Tilburg, November 2018. ©2018 Association for Computational Linguistics

human entertainment purposes, and can ultimately have some humour value, and thus be seen as punning riddles. If we see them as jokes, following Attardo (2008)'s classification, SECO falls under the first type, as it presents a humorous plot (question) with a punchline (answer).

As in JAPE (Binsted and Ritchie, 1994), riddle generation may follow different implemented models, all resorting to a (lexical-semantic) knowledge base (KB), in order to acquire features of given lexicalised concepts. A parallelism can roughly be made between our approach for generating riddles and the common architecture of a NLG system (Reiter and Dale, 2000), as it encompasses the following steps:

- **Model Instantiation & Feature Acquisition** (roughly, Content Determination): sets the model and exploits the KB for a combination of initial concept and related features;
- **Riddle Creation** (roughly, Microplanning): selects the appropriate words for denoting different types of feature and sets how the selected combination is going to be presented as text, i.e., as a definition or as a question-answering pair;
- **Rendering** (Surface Realisation): renders the combination as text, after some adaptations that make it more natural.

This section describes the previous steps in more detail and ends with some examples.

3.1 Model Instantiation & Features

All generation models implemented start with an initial concept with two detachable parts (c_1, c_2), either lexicalised as a compound (e.g., *human rights*) or a single word that, based on its orthography, may be divided in two (e.g., *knowledge=know+ledge*). Each part is considered individually and features are retrieved from the KB, some involving the first part of the concept (in set F_1), others the second part (F_2). Features are represented as triples of the kind a $relatedTo$ b, where a and b are words and $relatedTo$ is the name of a semantic relation between meanings of a and b (e.g., *animal* hypernymOf *dog*). As such, every feature in $f_1 \in F_1$ and $f_2 \in F_2$ will consist of a relation involving, respectively, c_1 and c_2.

- $F_1 : \forall(x, relatedTo, y) \in F_1$
  $\rightarrow (x = c_1 \wedge y = fw_1) \vee (x = fw_1 \wedge y = c_1)$
- $F_2 : \forall(x, relatedTo, y) \in F_2$
  $\rightarrow (x = c_2 \wedge y = fw_2) \vee (x = fw_2 \wedge y = c_2)$

After this, features $f_1 \in F_1$ are paired with features $f_2 \in F_2$. The result is a set of combinations of the initial concept with pairs $\{fw_1, fw_2\}$. Figure 1 illustrates this step, with d_1 and d_2 representing textual descriptions of the features that connect c_1 to fw_1 and c_2 to fw_2, respectively.

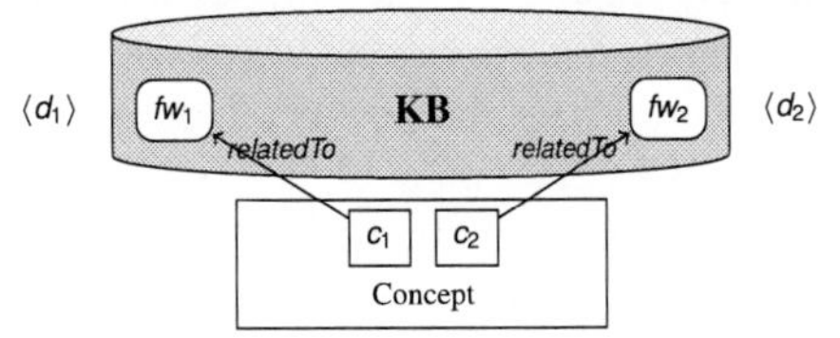

Figure 1: Feature acquisition

3.1.1 Lexical Resources

Two lexical resources are used by all the riddle generation models and are thus essential to this work. A **lexical-semantic knowledge base (KB)** with relation instances that occur in at least three out of ten semantic networks for Portuguese, including dictionaries, wordnets and ConceptNet (see Gonçalo Oliveira (2018) for additional details), that has a total of 45,510 instances, covering a rich set of relation types (see section 3.2), and is used by all the models.

A **morphology lexicon** (Ranchhod et al., 1999) with more than 900,000 Portuguese word forms, their part-of-speech and other grammatical information. It is used by the models to handle inflections and can also be used as a source of words (e.g., in models based on a single word).

3.1.2 Implemented Models

Inspired both by the schemata of JAPE (Binsted and Ritchie, 1994) and by the kind of jokes that Portuguese children use to make, we implemented six riddle generation models. A key difference is that they produce riddles in Portuguese and are thus constrained by the available lexical resources in this language. All models instantiate the generic model of Figure 1, but follow a different intuition, reflected in their input and, for the last two, on the features explored.

Reinterpretation of compounds (RC): given a known noun+adjective compound (c_1 + c_2), features are acquired for each of its words individually, and used to (re-)define it. Our intuition is that the meaning of the compounds is more than just

Proceedings of the 3rd Workshop on Computational Creativity and Natural Language Generation, pages 17–25,
Tilburg, November 2018. ©2018 Association for Computational Linguistics

the sum of the meanings of both of their words, which may result in unexpected associations, possibly perceived as incongruent, and thus humour-prone. The input for this model was a list of 180 Portuguese noun+adjective compounds (Ramisch et al., 2016), with instances such as *água doce* (fresh water), *mau-humor* (bad mood), or *primeira mão* (first hand/leg).

New compounds (NC): explores the idea that humour may result from new words with familiar sounds (homophony, paronymy). It generates new compounds from all pairs of valid words with an edit distance of 1 letter to the original compounds, and then works as RC. With the same list as RC, instances like *amido oculto* (occult starch), *véu aberto* (open veil) or *primeiro pano* (first cloth) are obtained, respectively from *amigo oculto* (occult friend), *céu aberto* (open sky) and *primeiro plano* (first plan).

Reinterpretation of words (RW): instead of compounds, this model is based on single words, interpreted as a blend of two. This often leads to an unexpected meaning, attributed to the word, again perceived as incongruent, thus increasing the humour potential. Target words are in the lexicon and have the form $w_1 w_2$, where w_1 and w_2 are character sequences that are also in the lexicon. Instances of this kind include *malabar* (juggle) — interpreted as *mala+bar* (suitcase+bar) —, *centralidade* (centrality) — interpreted as *central+idade* (central+age) —, or *restolho* (stubble) — interpreted as *resto+olho* (rest+eye).

New blends (NB): analogous to NC, but in respect to RW instead of RC. Before trying to reinterpret words, a small change is made in their orthography, according to a short handcrafted list of possible character sequence replacements that do not change the sound of the word excessively. Those are sequences like {*on*, *un*, *ão*}, {*i*, *e*} or {*r*, *l*}, which can be replaced in lexicon words and result in instances such as *fundasom* — obtained from *fundação* (foundation) and split into *funda* (catapult) and *som* (sound) — , *bombesta* — from *bombista* (bomber), split into *bom* (good) and besta (beast) — , or *calavela* — from *caravela* (caravel), split into *cala* (shut) and *vela* (sail). Each part of the instance (c_1 and c_2) must be in the lexicon, and thus be valid, but their blend ($w_1 w_2$) is not necessarily an existing word. The result is a new concept with a sound that resembles a known one, interpreted as the blend of two other (often unrelated) concepts.

Partial antonyms (PA): assumes that the orthography of some words starts or ends with the antonym of another and that novel antonyms may result from changing the start/end of those words with its antonym. Instances of this kind include *pormenor* (detail) — where *menor* (smaller) is antonym of *maior* (bigger), resulting in novel antonym *pormaior* —, or *diante* (in front of) — where *dia* (day) is antonym of *noite* (night), resulting in antonym *noitente*. To avoid atypical words, some considerations on how syllables are formed and their limits are made. For instance, with a direct replacement, the antonyms of *sair*, *assalto*, *salvo* and *negativo* would be, respectively, *saandar*, *assbaixo*, *snegro* and *negpassivo*. With those considerations, they become *sandar*, *asbaixo*, *salnegro* and *nepassivo*.

Antonymy Blend (AB): revisits the idea that, due to their orthography, some words can be interpreted as a blend of other two. Yet, it is focused on those where both parts (c_1, c_2) have an antonym. This is used in the generation of novel antonyms, such as *odiar-atingir* (hate-reach) — for *amarfalhar* (to crumple), interpreted as *amar+falhar* (to love+to fail) —, *sombra-ilegal* (illegal-shadow), for *solícito* (solicitous), interpreted as *sol+lícito* (sun+lawful) —, or *mau-mau* (bad-bad) — for *bombom* (candy), interpreted as *bom+bom* (good+good).

3.2 Riddle Creation

Riddles have to be conveyed in natural language in a way that the relation between the concept and the features is understood. Depending on the types of feature, the text to clarify the relation is set, before selecting how the riddle is to be presented.

3.2.1 Feature Description

In the KB, relation instances connect words according to one of their meanings, but different meanings of the same word are not explicitly identified. Though unintentionally, this enables the selection of less expected meanings because the chance of selecting exactly the same meaning a word has in a compound is low, especially when the global meaning is not the sum of the parts (c_1, c_2) meaning.

As the relations used are present in at least three other resources, they are generally well-known and consensual. If this constraint is dropped, more features can be extracted, though less immedi-

Proceedings of the 3rd Workshop on Computational Creativity and Natural Language Generation, pages 17–25,
Tilburg, November 2018. ©2018 Association for Computational Linguistics

ate. The risk of using incorrect features is also higher, because most available semantic networks for Portuguese are created (semi-)automatically, with minimal or no curation.

From the available relations, we identified a subset of types that could be used as features. Some of those types are listed in Table 1, together with their frequency in the KB, and the text of their description, in Portuguese, to be used in the riddles, followed by a rough English translation. As only synonymy and antonymy are symmetrical relations, some types have different descriptions, depending on the position of the concept word (c_i) and feature word (fw_i) in the relation. There are also relations for which no text is necessary besides the feature word itself. Finally, if fw_i is a noun, it will be preceded by an indefinite article (*um*, for masculine, *uma* for feminine).

#	Relation	arg$_1$	arg$_2$	Description (d_i)
7,538	adj-synonymOf	fw_i / c_i	c_i / fw_i	*o que é* fw_i (what is fw_i)
353	adj-antonymOf	fw_i / c_i	c_i / fw_i	*o que não é/está* fw_i (what is not fw_i)
157	v-antonymOf	fw_i / c_i	c_i / fw_i	*o que não* fw_i (what does not fw_i)
4,035	hypernymOf	fw_i	c_i	fw_i
590	adj-saidAbout-n	c_i	fw_i	fw_i
		fw_i	c_i	*o que é* fw_i
100	n-partOf-adj	c_i	fw_i	*o que é* fw_i
		fw_i	c_i	fw_i
58	n-partOf-n	c_i	fw_i	*uma parte de* fw_i (a part of fw_i)
		fw_i	c_i	*o que tem* fw_i (what has fw_i)
		fw_i	c_i	*o que tem* fw_i
110	v-purposeOf-n	c_i	fw_i	*a finalidade de* fw_i
		fw_i	c_i	*o que serve para* fw_i
1,572	v-causes-n	c_i	fw_i	fw_i
		fw_i	c_i	*o efeito de* fw_i (the effect of fw_i)

Table 1: Feature types and textual description

3.2.2 Presentation Mode Selection

Each combination of an initial concept and related features can be presented in different (hard-coded) ways, such as those in Table 2. Those include a definition (**DEF**); a question with two features for which the initial concept is the answer (**FC**); a question with the initial concept for which the features are in the answer (**CF**); or questions that ask for the opposite of the initial concept / pair of features, answered with a pair of features / initial concept (**OP1**, **OP2**).

3.3 Rendering

The riddle is finally rendered as a text with the concept and the features description. Yet to make text more natural, additional adaptations have to be made, depending on the presentation mode and

ID	Template
DEF	$\langle concept \rangle$`:` $d_1 f_1$ `e` $d_2 f_2$
FC	`Que resulta do cruzamento entre` $d_1 f_1$ `e` $d_2 f_2$ `?` $\langle concept \rangle$`.` (What do you get when you cross ... ?)
CF	`O que significa` $\langle concept \rangle$`?` $d_1 f_1$ `e` $d_2 f_2$`.` (What does ... mean?)
OP1	`Qual é o contrário de` $\langle concept \rangle$`?` f_1 f_2`.` (What is the opposite of ... ?)
OP2	`Qual é o contrário de` $f_1 f_2$`?` $\langle concept \rangle$`.` (What is the opposite of ... ?)

Table 2: Presentation templates for riddles

on the kind of features, namely:

- A1 Noun features should appear before other features.
- A2 If one feature is a noun and the other an adjective, the description of the adjective is removed, because it is clear enough that the adjective is modifying the noun.
- A3 If one feature is a noun and the other is an adjective, the adjective must have the same gender as the noun and is inflected according to the lexicon.
- A4 If both features are nouns, *que é* (what is) is added before the second, and both can be interpreted as 'co-hypernyms.'
- A5 If both features are adjectives, the description of the second is removed.
- A6 If one feature is an adjective but can also be used as a noun, it is used as a noun.
- A7 When necessary, the conjunction *e* (and) is added between the feature descriptions.

Adaptations A1 to A5 apply to the presentation modes DEF, CF and OP1; A6 is applied to FC; and A7 is applied to all.

3.4 Dissected Examples

To illustrate the previous steps, we present some examples of generated riddles. Consider, for example, the concept *direitos humanos* (human rights), in the compounds list, for which the features acquired from the KB include:

direito synonymOf *liso* (right, flat)
direito synonymOf *plano* (right, plane)
direito antonymOf *torto* (right, bent)
humano saidAbout *homem* (human, man)

From those, the riddles in Table 3 could be the result of the RC model. The instantiation of the generic model that results in the fifth riddle is depicted in Figure 2.

Despite different possible ways for presenting the riddles, a default one was set for each model, namely: FC for RC, except when one of the features is an antonym, with OP2 being used instead; CF for NC, RW, NB; OP1 for PA and AB. Table 4 has examples of riddles generated by each model, covering every rendering adaptation, and including a rough English translation.

Proceedings of the 3rd Workshop on Computational Creativity and Natural Language Generation, pages 17–25,
Tilburg, November 2018.

Riddle	Pres.	Adapt.
direitos humanos: um homem liso. (human rights: a flat man)	DEF	A1, A2
direitos humanos: um homem plano.	DEF	A1, A2
direitos humanos: um homem que não é/está torto.	DEF	A1, A2
Que resulta do cruzamento entre o que é liso e um homem? direitos humanos.	FC	A7
Que resulta do cruzamento entre um plano e um homem? direitos humanos. (What do you get when you cross a plane and a man? human rights.)	FC	A6
Qual é o contrário de homem torto? direitos humanos.	OP2	A1, A2
O que significa direitos humanos? um homem liso.	CF	A1, A2
O que significa direitos humanos? um homem plano.	CF	A1, A2
O que significa direitos humanos? um homem que não é/está torto. (What does human rights mean? a man that is not bent.)	CF	A1

Table 3: Riddles generated for the concept *direitos humanos* (human rights)

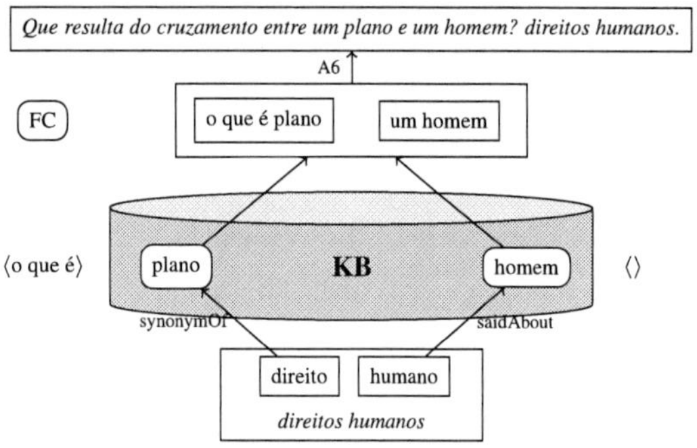

Figure 2: Instantiation of the RC model with the expression *direitos humanos*

4 Validation

The assessment of the riddles includes highly subjective aspects, namely humour. Also given that the riddles were created for human consumption, we decided to validate our results with the opinion of a general audience. For this purpose, a sample of produced riddles was generated and deployed to the Figure-Eight[1] crowdsourcing platform, in a job called *Adivinhas em Português* (Riddles in Portuguese), to be answered by human judges from Portugal and Brazil, paid for this purpose. This section describes the assessed aspects, how the sample was generated, and discusses the obtained results.

4.1 Assessed Aspects

Since our goal was to produce novel riddles, ideally with humour value, both novelty and humour potential had to be assessed. We also wanted to know if the audience could understand the riddle and if it actually made surprising associations. Subjects were not informed that the riddles had been produced automatically. They were just instructed to use a 5-point Likert scale for scoring the four aspects, given the descriptions in Table 5.

4.2 Validation Sample

A 300-riddle sample was created for validation, all rendered with the default presentation mode (see section 3.2.2) and randomly selected from the top-150 riddles by each model, ranked roughly based on the commonality and representativeness of their features. Our intuition was that using more common words in the riddle would improve its understanding. So, the higher the frequency of their features in the CETEMPúblico (Rocha and Santos, 2000) corpus, the higher the rank. Yet, features should be as representative as possible of the concept. For instance, asking for the hyponym of a word with too many hyponyms (e.g., person, plant, instrument) decreases solvability, an aspect considered by Labutov and Lipson (2012). So, the rank was penalised according to the number of other words related the same way as the concept is to the used features.

4.3 Results

Each riddle had the four aspects rated by three subjects, enabling us to compute the agreement on answers we knew to be subjective. Table 6 shows the global results of this validation. Considering the sample and rated aspects, it shows the proportion of answers with scores from 1 to 5, three statistical measures and the judge agreement. The latter confirms the subjectivity involved in this validation. Curiously, humour potential is where agreement is higher, due to its lower average rating. Only 6% of the riddles clearly made the subject laugh, but subjects also say that more than 30% could make someone else laugh. On the other hand, 30% of the riddles would make no one laugh. We are not completely satisfied with the results on this aspect but, given the underlying subjectivity, we still think they are interesting and provide a baseline for further iterations of SECO.

On average, interpretation was accessible, which means that most riddles could be understood, but only after a second reading. Both surprise and, especially, novelty were rated higher than interpretation. This means that the riddles use some unexpected associations and the majority is

[1] `https://www.figure-eight.com/`

Proceedings of the 3rd Workshop on Computational Creativity and Natural Language Generation, pages 17–25,
Tilburg, November 2018.

Model	Initial concept	Features	Description	Adaptations	Riddle
NC	primeiro ministro primeiro sinistro (used)	*primeiro* synonymOf *inicial* *sinistro* synonymOf *mau*	*o que é inicial* *o que é mau*	A5, A7	*O que significa primeiro sinistro?* *O que é inicial e mau.*
[en]	prime minister prime sinister	prime, initial sinister, bad	what is early what is bad		What does prime sinister mean? What is initial and bad.
RW	eleitoral	*eleito* synonymOf *escolhido* *oral* saidAbout *boca*	*o que é escolhido* *uma boca*	A1, A2, A3	*O que significa eleitoral?* *Uma boca escolhida.*
[en]	electoral	elected, chosen oral, mouth	a mouth what is chosen		What does electoral mean? A chosen mouth.
NB	barrenar barrenal (used)	*sala* hypernymOf *bar* *renal* saidAbout *rim*	*uma sala* *um rim*	A4	*O que significa barrenal?* *Uma sala que é um rim.*
[en]	drill bar+renal	room, bar renal, kidney	a room a kidney		What does 'bar+renal' mean? A room that is a kidney.
PA	bombeiro	*bom* antonymOf *mau*	*bombeiro*	–	*Qual o contrário de bombeiro? maubeiro.*
[en]	fireman	good (=bom), bad			What is the opposite of fireman? 'bad*beiro*'
AB	procurador	*procura* antonymOf *oferta* *dor* antonymOf *alegria*	*procurador*	–	*Qual o contrário de procurador?* *oferta-alegria.*
[en]	procurator	demand (=procura), supply pain (=dor), joy			What is the opposite of procurator (demand-pain)? supply-joy.

Table 4: Examples for each riddle generation model

Interpretation		
1	Hard	the riddle is impossible to understand, no matter how you try;
3	Accessible	after reading it more than once and thinking about it, the riddle can be understood;
5	Easy	the riddle was understood the first time you read it.
Surprise		
1	Too obvious	the riddle is too basic or literal;
3	Somewhat unexpected	the riddle makes some interesting associations;
5	Unexpected	the riddle makes unexpected associations, you had never thought of it and would never think of.
Novelty		
1	Known	the riddle is already known by you;
3	Familiar	the riddle sounds like some other riddle you know;
5	Novel	the riddle is unknown and different from those you know.
Humour potential		
1	None	the riddle will make no one laugh;
3	Some	the riddle did not make you laugh, but could make someone laugh (child or adult);
5	Great	the riddle made you laugh and has a great humour potential.

Table 5: Assessed aspects and their description

effectively novel and previously unknown by the subjects, which was one of our goals.

Table 7 has a selection of riddles. A rough English translation was included for each but, in most cases, it hardly transmits the actual meaning in Portuguese. The selection highlights riddles that stand out in some aspect, including riddles with high novelty (1–3) and humour potential (4–6). Some riddles with low interpretation (7 and others not in the table) are longer than the average, which may explain this rate, but for others we have found no explanation besides, possibly, laziness (8, 9). To stress the underlying subjectivity, we included riddles where subjects highly disagreed on the humour potential (10–14), for which the three given ratings on this aspect are shown. One of them (10) is also one of the few with very low novelty. This is a possible cause of disagreement, as many people will not find a joke so funny once they heard it for the first time. On the other hand, this shows that SECO may generate a minority of familiar riddles, originally created by humans. The remaining riddles in the table are a personal selection with humour rated higher than average.

Score	Interp	Surp	Novel	Humour
1	11.8%	8.0%	6.7%	28.7%
2	20.4%	10.7%	12.4%	24.6%
3	23.7%	29.3%	24.8%	25.0%
4	22.6%	33.0%	25.1%	15.7%
5	21.6%	19.0%	31.0%	6.1%
Mean ($\bar{x}$)	3.2±1.2	3.4±1.1	3.6±1.2	2.5±1.2
Mode (*Mo*)	3	4	5	1
Median (*Md*)	3	4	4	2
Agreement	54%	59%	56%	62%

Table 6: Global results of human validation

On a side note, 42% of the answers were from Portugal and 58% from Brazil. The average score for surprise and humour was the same for both countries and, although Portuguese judges rated interpretation and novelty 0.2 points higher, standard deviations are large.

Table 8 organises the global results according to the generation model. Due both to the high standard deviations and because we are using Likert scales, it is focused on the mode and median. It is clear that not all models result in riddles with the same quality. AB riddles seem to be the easiest to understand, the lowest surprise is for RW, and the highest novelty is for NB, PA and AB. On humour, two models should be highlighted for producing riddles with higher average potential: RC and AB. Yet, so far we have no better explanation than a higher acceptance of this kind of riddles as

Proceedings of the 3rd Workshop on Computational Creativity and Natural Language Generation, pages 17–25,
Tilburg, November 2018. ©2018 Association for Computational Linguistics

#	$\overline{Interp}$	$\overline{Surp}$	$\overline{Nov}$	$\overline{Hum}$	Riddle
1	4.0	2.0	5.0	2.0	*Qual é o contrário de dialiso? noite-áspera.* (What is the opposite of dialyse (day+flat)? night-rough)
2	2.0	4.0	5.0	1.0	*O que significa numero? o que é descoberto e simples.* (What does number (naked+mere) mean? what is uncovered and simple.)
3	2.3	4.7	5.0	3.0	*Qual é o contrário de prevenir? prevandar.* (What is the opposite of to prevent ('preven'+go)? 'prev'+come.)
4	5.0	2.7	3.3	4.7	*Qual é o contrário de frequente? frefrio.* (What is the opposite of frequent ('fre'+hot)? 'fre'+cold.)
5	4.3	2.7	3.0	4.7	*Qual é o contrário de atropelado? alvo-vestido.* (What is the opposite of ran over (dark+naked)? white-dressed.)
6	4.7	2.7	3.3	4.7	*Qual é o contrário de malbarato? bem-caro.* (What is the opposite of waste (bad+cheap)? quite-expensive.)
7	1.7	4.3	4.0	1.0	*O que significa enfiamento? a finalidade de uma agulheta que é uma parte de rosto.* (What does threading (to thread/stick+chin) mean? the purpose of a needle that is a part of the face.)
8	1.3	4.0	4.7	1.3	*Qual é o contrário de pagamento seco? sinal verde.* (What is the opposite of dry payment? green light (sign).)
9	1.7	3.3	3.7	1.3	*Qual é o contrário de reclamar? reclodiar.* (What is the opposite of to complain ('rec'+to love)? 'rec'+to hate.)
10	5.0	1.0	1.7	[4, 5, 1]	*Qual é o contrário de pormenor? pormaior.* (What is the opposite of pormenor ('por'+smaller)? 'por'+bigger.)
11	3.0	3.7	4.3	[5, 2, 1]	*Que resulta do cruzamento entre uma unidade e um indiferente? pé-frio.* (What do you get when you cross a unit and an indifferent? cold feet.)
12	4.0	4.0	4.0	[4, 1, 5]	*Qual é o contrário de virtual? irtual.* (What is the opposite of virtual (come+'tual')? go+'tual'.)
13	3.7	4.7	4.3	[5, 3, 1]	*Qual é o contrário de bemole? mal-duro.* (What is the opposite of flat (note, well+soft)? bad-hard.)
14	2.7	3.3	3.3	[1, 5, 2]	*O que significa abalesto? um prolongamento que é ligeiro.* (What does flap+agile mean? an extension that is light.)
15	3.3	3.7	3.7	4.0	*Que resulta do cruzamento entre um sentido e o que é consistente? vista grossa.* (What do you get when you cross a sense with what is consistent? thick sight.)
16	4.3	3.3	4.3	3.3	*O que significa cãotributo? um pagamento canino.* (What does 'dogtribute' mean? a canine payment.)
17	4.3	3.3	3.3	4.0	*O que significa pronto forte? o que é imediato e não é/está fraco.* (What does prompt strong mean? what is immediate and is not weak.)
18	3.0	4.0	4.0	3.3	*O que significa ecoponto? um som que serve para coser.* (What does ecopoint (echo+point) mean? a sound for sewing.)
19	4.7	3.0	3.0	4.0	*Qual é o contrário de animal? anibem.* (What is the opposite of animal ('ani'+bad)? 'ani'+well.)
20	3.3	4.0	4.3	3.7	*Qual é o contrário de procurador? oferta-alegria.* (What is the opposite of procurator (demand+pain)? supply-joy.)

Table 7: Selection of generation riddles with their average validation scores

jokes by the majority of the subjects. For instance, the FC presentation, used by the RC model, relies on a linguistic construction common in jokes.

Aspect	Meas	Model					
		RC	NC	RW	NB	PA	AB
Interpret	Mo	4	4	3	3	5	5
	Md	3	3	3	3	3	4
Surprise	Mo	4	4	3	4	4	4
	Md	4	4	4	4	4	3
Novelty	Mo	4	4	3	5	5	5
	Md	4	4	3	4	4	4
Humour	Mo	3	1	1	1	1	3
	Md	3	2	2	2	2	3
Total in sample		32	45	50	52	59	62

Table 8: Human validation according to model

5 Conclusion

We have described six models for generating novel riddles, in Portuguese, from a knowledge-base, incorporated in the system SECO. Even though human validation confirmed the subjectivity of their appreciation, overall, subjects found the riddles accessible, surprising, and novel, though with a low humour potential, especially for riddles produced by four of those models. We also highlight that the generated riddles are in Portuguese, a relevant contribution, given that, to the best of our knowledge, there was no such previous work of this kind on this language.

The ability of understanding and, in this specific case, using humour, are important steps towards making artificial agents more natural. In principle, the proposed models could be integrated in one of such agents. We have plans for a Twitter bot that will use them, but are still testing different ways of selecting riddles appropriate for a given context (e.g., recent news / top trends).

Furthermore, we aim at better analysing the results of the human validation including, for instance, correlations between different rated aspects. Using the same criteria for scoring riddles that humans actually use would provide useful insights, but it would require a great number of "consensual" riddles of the tackled kinds, which is highly unlikely. In further iterations of SECO, we will devise the inclusion of alternative models of riddles or humour (e.g., *What's the difference between...*) and we plan to study different ways of ranking the produced riddles automatically, not only based on commonality and representativeness, but also on humour-relevant features (e.g., incongruity, presence of taboo words).

Proceedings of the 3rd Workshop on Computational Creativity and Natural Language Generation, pages 17–25,
Tilburg, November 2018.

References

Salvatore Attardo. 2008. A primer for the linguistics of humor. In Victor Raskin, editor, *The Primer of Humor Research*, chapter 3, pages 101–156. De Gruyter Mouton.

Kim Binsted and Graeme Ritchie. 1994. An implemented model of punning riddles. In *Procs 12th National Conf. on AI*, volume 1 of *AAAI '94*, pages 633–638, Menlo Park, CA, USA. AAAI Press.

Paloma Galvan, Virginia Francisco, Raquel Hervás, and Gonzalo Mendez. 2016. Riddle generation using word associations. In *Proceedings of 10th International Conference on Language Resources and Evaluation (LREC 2016)*. ELRA.

Robert A. Georges and Alan Dundes. 1963. Towards a structural definition of the riddle. *Journal of American Folklore*, 76(300):111—18.

Hugo Gonçalo Oliveira and Ricardo Rodrigues. 2018. A set of procedures attempting at the generation of verbal humor in Portuguese. In *Proceedings of 9th International Conference on Computational Creativity*, ICCC 2018, page 307, Salamanca, Spain. ACC.

Hugo Gonçalo Oliveira. 2018. A survey on Portuguese lexical knowledge bases: Contents, comparison and combination. *Information*, 9(2):34.

Hugo Gonçalo Oliveira, Diogo Costa, and Alexandre Pinto. 2016. One does not simply produce funny memes! – explorations on the automatic generation of Internet humor. In *Proceedings of 7th International Conference on Computational Creativity*, ICCC 2016, Paris, France.

Hugo Gonçalo Oliveira and Ricardo Rodrigues. 2018b. Explorando a geração automática de adivinhas em português. *Linguamática*, 10(1):3–18.

Ivan Guerrero, Ben Verhoeven, Francesco Barbieri, Pedro Martins, and Rafael Perez y Perez. 2015. TheRiddlerBot: A next step on the ladder towards creative Twitter bots. In *Proceedings of 6th International Conference on Computational Creativity*, ICCC 2015, pages 315–322, Park City, Utah. Brigham Young University.

Igor Labutov and Hod Lipson. 2012. Humor as circuits in semantic networks. In *Proceedings of the 50th Annual Meeting of the Association for Computational Linguistics: Short Papers - Volume 2*, ACL '12, pages 150–155, Stroudsburg, PA, USA. ACL Press.

Ruli Manurung, Graeme Ritchie, Helen Pain, Annalu Waller, Dave O'Mara, and Rolf Black. 2008. The construction of a pun generator for language skills development. *Applied AI*, 22(9):841–869.

Rada Mihalcea and Carlo Strapparava. 2006. Learning to laugh (automatically): Computational models for humor recognition. *Computational Intelligence*, 22(2):126–142.

Paul de Palma and E. Judith Weiner. 1992. Riddles: Accessibility and knowledge representation. In *COLING 1992 Volume 4: The 15th International Conference on Computational Linguistics*.

Pedro Pinto, João Ramalhinho, and Gonçalo Castro. 2017. *O Caderno das Piadas Secas – 500 Tentativas de ter graça*. Manuscrito Editora.

Carlos Ramisch, Silvio Cordeiro, Leonardo Zilio, Marco Idiart, and Aline Villavicencio. 2016. How naked is the naked truth? a multilingual lexicon of nominal compound compositionality. In *Proceedings of the 54th Annual Meeting of the Association for Computational Linguistics (Volume 2: Short Papers)*, pages 156–161, Berlin, Germany. ACL Press.

Elisabete Ranchhod, Cristina Mota, and Jorge Baptista. 1999. A computational lexicon of Portuguese for automatic text parsing. In *Proceedings of SIGLEX99 Workshop: Standardizing Lexical Resources*. ACL Press.

Ehud Reiter and Robert Dale. 2000. *Building Natural Language Generation Systems*. Cambridge University Press, New York, NY, USA.

G. Ritchie, D. O'Mara, K. Binsted, R. Manurung, S. Coulson, B. Bergen, A. Waller, O. Stock, C. Strapparava, H. Pain, and A. Nijholt. 2006. Computational humor. *IEEE Intelligent Systems*, 21:59–69.

Paulo Alexandre Rocha and Diana Santos. 2000. CETEMPúblico: Um corpus de grandes dimensões de linguagem jornalística portuguesa. In *V Encontro para o processamento computacional da língua portuguesa escrita e falada (PROPOR 2000)*, pages 131–140, São Paulo. ICMC/USP.

Jonas Sjöbergh and Kenji Araki. 2007. Automatically creating word-play jokes in Japanese. In *Procs. of NL-178*, pages 91–95, Nagoya, Japan.

Oliviero Stock and Carlo Strapparava. 2006. Laughing with HAHAcronym, a computational humor system. In *Proceedings of 21st National Conference on AI - Volume 2*, AAAI'06, pages 1675–1678. AAAI Press.

Stella E. O. Tagnin. 2005. O humor como quebra da convencionalidade. *Revista Brasileira de Lingüística Aplicada*, 5(1):247–257.

Alessandro Valitutti, Antoine Doucet, Jukka Toivanen, and Hannu Toivonen. 2016. Computational generation and dissection of lexical replacement humor. *Natural Language Engineering*, 22(5):1–23.

Diyi Yang, Alon Lavie, Chris Dyer, and Eduard Hovy. 2015. Humor recognition and humor anchor extraction. In *Proceedings of the 2015 Conference on Empirical Methods in Natural Language Processing*, pages 2367–2376, Lisbon, Portugal. ACL Press.

Proceedings of the 3rd Workshop on Computational Creativity and Natural Language Generation, pages 17–25,
Tilburg, November 2018.

Content Determination for Chess as a Source for Suspenseful Narratives

Richard Doust
Independent Researcher
Open University, UK
richard.doust@gmail.com

Pablo Gervás
Facultad de Informática
Instituto de Tecnologîa del Conocimiento
Universidad Complutense de Madrid
pgervas@ucm.es

Abstract

In this paper, we explore a way of viewing a chess game as a narrative. Using the model of suspense described in Doust (2015), Doust and Piwek (2017) and Doust (2017), we derive a fluctuating step-by-step prediction of the suspense level evoked by a series of steps in a particular chess endgame scenario. Based on these predictions, particular variations from a given set-up of the game may be chosen to induce a story for the game that optimises the value of the suspense perceived by an observer following the narrative that results from the game. This provides a content determination strategy for a system that constructs chess games specifically to support suspenseful stories.

1 Introduction

When an author sits down to write a story, one possible goal in his mind may be to evoke feelings of suspense in the prospective reader. To achieve this, the writer plays both with the content that he includes in his story and the order in which it is presented to the reader. Some recent efforts in the computational study of narrative have focused in the way this inducement of feelings of suspense may be achieved (Delatorre and Arfè, 2015; Delatorre et al., 2016). In this paper, we explore a possible way of selecting between possible continuations of a chess game such that the story of its telling be such that it evokes a desirable amount of suspense.

The game of chess – being a simplified model of a world that includes conflict between opposing factions (black and white) constituted by individuals (pieces) that carry out actions (moves) driven by an illusion of purpose (the strategy of each player) – has already been used as a case study for computational studies on the construction of narrative (Gervás, 2014; Delatorre and Gervás, 2014; Gervás, 2018a,b).

In this paper, we explore a way of viewing a chess game as a narrative. Using the model of suspense described in Doust (2015), Doust and Piwek (2017) and Doust (2017), we derive a fluctuating step-by-step prediction of the suspense level evoked by a series of steps in a particular chess endgame scenario. Based on these predictions, particular variations from a given set-up of the game may be chosen to induce a story for the game that optimises the value of the suspense perceived by an observer following the narrative that results from the game. This provides a content determination strategy for a system that constructs chess games specifically to support suspenseful stories.

1.1 Design choices

In searching for suitable domains to explore the potential and the validity of our model, the chess world has the advantages of simplicity, clarity and closure. This is especially true in the endgame phase where there are fewer pieces on the board and the available options are easy to see and predict. In the endgame, the King and Pawns have the advantage of only moving one square at a time. Their movement has a certain linearity. The goal of queening a pawn is also a very clear endpoint for a pawn. For these reasons we have limited ourselves to a particular chess endgame with only Kings and Pawns on the board. If the model is successful, other more complex setups with additional pieces could be considered.

In extrapolating a narrative from a board game or indeed any sport, there are several options. One of these would be to consider the individual stories of the different pieces. For the chess example we could create a narrative of the pawn's self-realisation in becoming a queen. We could use terms such as far, near, close, within firing range to simulate the approximate non-omniscient knowl-

Proceedings of the 3rd Workshop on Computational Creativity and Natural Language Generation, pages 26–33,
Tilburg, November 2018.

edge or field of view that a piece has of the other pieces on the board. In this way, we could tell the suspenseful and surprising story of the events that happen to a given piece. In such an approach, the unpredictability that is essential to narrative would be achievable because the piece in question might not be aware beforehand of a different piece's sudden appearance in its field of view.

In this paper however, we follow the perhaps more usual idea of the suspenseful and surprising story derived from the movement of the pieces that is understood by a viewer of the game who observes both sides, white and black, and maybe supports one of the sides. In such an approach, however, it would appear to be harder to model the unpredictability needed to create a model of narrative, as all moves are visible and, theoretically at least, calculable by the observer. However, we will be simulating a non-expert observer with certain limits to its analytical powers, and this will enable us to simulate a narrative-like process with a degree of unpredictability from a series of chess moves.

2 Related Work

This section reviews existing studies on computational narrative based on chess and existing models of suspense.

2.1 Computational Narrative Studies based on Chess

The use of a chess game as a reference world on which to developed basic mechanics of narrative composition had been explored in Gervás (2014), where a basic concept of a narrative thread is introduced similar to the ones used in this paper. The evaluation of the perception of suspense over a chess game was addressed in Delatorre and Gervás (2014), using simple models of the level of threat perceived by each faction. Elementary models for proposing possible plot structures to account for a selected sequence of moves out of the record of a complete chess game are described in Gervás (2018a) and Gervás (2018b).

2.2 Computational Models of Suspense

Based on systematic reviews of existing cognitive models of suspense, the work described in Delatorre and Arfè (2015) and Delatorre et al. (2016) outlines a computational approach for measuring the suspense evoked by a given narrative, in terms of particular characteristics such as the relative strengths of the characters in opposition, the empathy inspired by different characters in the reader, and the props and settings for particular scenes.

2.3 Our narrative thread model of suspense

We now give a brief review of our narrative model of suspense as shown in Doust (2015), Doust and Piwek (2017) and Doust (2017).

Much research on computational models of narrative has often centred on use of detailed representations for character goals and plans – see for example Cavazza and Charles (2005). Also, approaches to suspense modelling often interlock with the concept of a story protagonist under some kind of threat – see for example, the suspense modelling in the SUSPENSER system Cheong and Young (2015) which attempts to maximise suspense by varying the number of potential actions of a central protagonist which could allow him or her to escape a threat.

In Doust (2015), we proposed a domain-independent model of suspense together with a method for measuring the suspensefulness of simple chronological narratives. By separating out emotional salience and character empathy considerations from informational and attentional processes at the heart of the suspense reaction, we constructed a modular definition of suspense.

In our model, which was inspired by the informal model presented in Brewer and Lichtenstein (1982), the concept of a *narrative thread* plays a pivotal role. Narrative threads model the reader's expectations about what might happen next in a given story. As a story is told, narrative threads are activated and de-activated. Different threads may point to conflicting events that are situated in the future. As more of the story is revealed, the moment of resolution of the conflict may appear more or less proximal in time. We capture this by formally defining the concept of *Imminence*. Imminence is based on the potential for upcoming storyworld events to conflict with one another and on the narrative proximity with these conflicts. It is the key factor in what we call conflict-based suspense[1].

For a given storyworld, our model requires a set of narrative threads. Each thread consists in a chronological list of potential events taken from the storyworld. In addition, we used a set of dis-

[1]Additionally, as the story is told, conflicting *interpretations* about certain events in the story may prevail. This led us to define a distinct second type of suspense which we call *revelatory suspense* which we will not examine in this paper.

Proceedings of the 3rd Workshop on Computational Creativity and Natural Language Generation, pages 26–33,
Tilburg, November 2018. ©2018 Association for Computational Linguistics

allowing ordered pairs of events to represents incompatible storyworld events. If one of a pair of disallowing events is told in the story, then the other event can no longer be told.

A story is then an ordered list of events taken from the storyworld that usually includes events from different narrative threads. Telling a story is equivalent to going through this ordered list of events one by one. Each new told event may have an effect on one or more narrative threads. Each narrative thread also has a *Told* and *Untold* event list. If the new story event matches a member of the *Untold* list of any narrative thread, then we move it (and all the events before it) into the thread's *Told* list. Additionally, the thread also becomes active (if previously, it was not). Finally, threads can get deactivated by certain events in the story according to a defined set of disallowing pairs of events.

3 Content Determination for Suspense-Inducing Stories based on Chess Games

We will use an endgame study by Réti as a working example (taken from Dvoretsky (2011, p. 29).

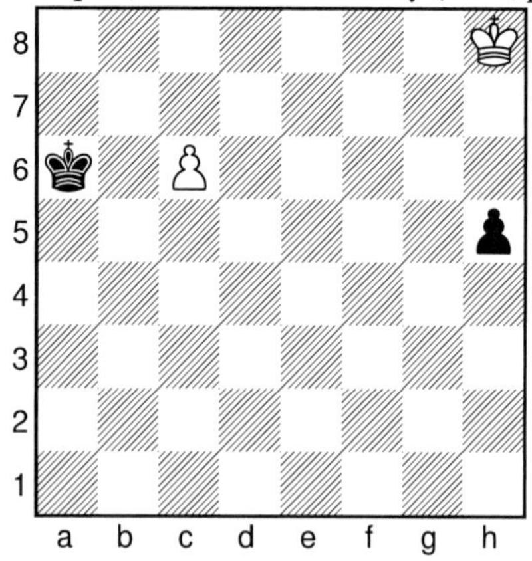

3.1 Deriving the narrative threads

It should ultimately be possible to derive the narrative threads inherent in a given chess position from automatic computational analysis of the position. However, we have chosen in this first approach to derive them by hand. This choice is linked to our strategy of focussing on a relatively simple endgame situation where, because we use only Kings and Pawns, the move choices more visibly resemble a thread-like structure.

Criteria for the identification of a narrative thread are that it has a clear start and end point. As we shall see, in the chess storyworld, a thread can often be usefully labelled with a goal-like description such as 'wants to take a piece', 'wants to stop a piece getting taken', 'wants to make a queen', etc. We inferred a set of narrative threads that we consider relevant for this chess position. We now show these on the chessboard.

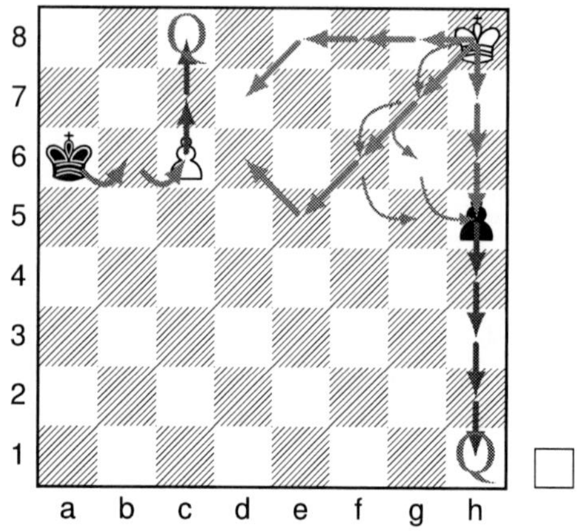

The black king has a thread of two steps culminating in the capture of the white pawn (grey arrows). The white pawn has a thread of two steps culminating in becoming a queen (blue arrows) and the black pawn has a thread of 4 steps to become a queen (purple arrows). The white king has two sets of threads: one set (red arrows) contains the more or less equivalent paths to try to catch the black pawn (currently 3 steps away), the other set (brown arrows) contains roughly equivalent paths to get close to the white pawn to stop it being taken by the black king (currently 4 steps away).

In Table 1, we show a sample of the threads in a table form.

Table 1: Narrative threads sample

Thread Name	Thread steps				
Black pawn	h5	h4	h3	h2	h1
White pawn	c6	c7	c8		
White king chases pawn	h8	h7	h6	h5	

Computationally, we use the following format for each thread: a Name, an Importance value, a sequence of Told events (or moves) and a sequence of as yet Untold events.

- arc(Name,Importance,[Told],[Untold])

To help to understand the overall structure and interlinking of these narrative threads, we now show some visual interpretations of the narrative threads

Proceedings of the 3rd Workshop on Computational Creativity and Natural Language Generation, pages 26–33,
Tilburg, November 2018. ©2018 Association for Computational Linguistics

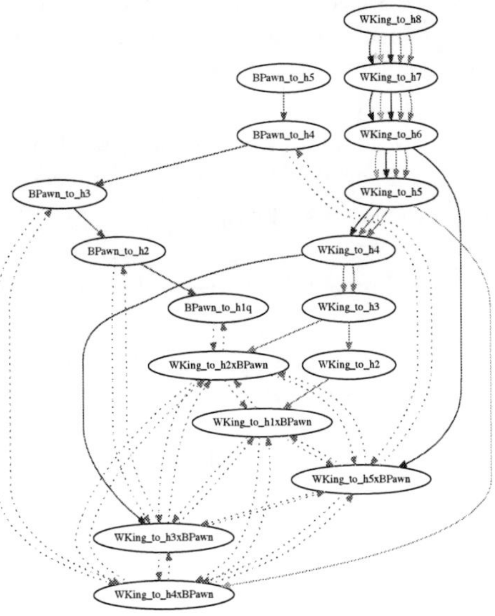

Figure 1: Narrative threads for the White King and Black Pawn

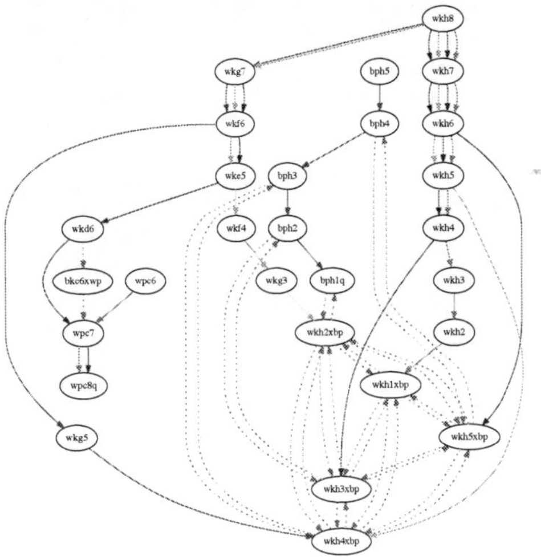

Figure 2: Narrative threads for the whole Réti position

for this chess position. First, we show the interaction between just the White King and the Black Pawn in Figure 1.

In this figure, each thread has its own colour. We can see that different threads can 'pass through' the same chess move. The red dotted lines identify the moves that disallow each other, that is, if one of these occurs, then the other can no longer occur in the game. These disallowing links are necessary to eliminate certain threads as soon as for example the pawn is captured.

Next, in order to give an idea of the global structure of our narrative thread systems, we show the complete system of narrative threads for this chess position (with abbreviated labels due to space) in Figure 2.

This global view also helps to see how the different threads are linked and where interesting narratives may lie. In this Figure, several threads for the White King link up to the square $e5^2$ and then split into two directions: one to protect the white pawn, the other to try to capture the black pawn. Indeed, this move turns out to be the key to solving the original study.

[2]In the Figure, this shown by the event $wke5$ third down from the top in the centre

3.2 Modelling the reader's predicted reactions: the suspense algorithm

3.3 Modelling our observer

We will make some assumptions that the observer of our game is a rather naive beginner who does not calculate the interaction of the narrative threads in absolute terms, but rather has a feel for each narrative thread's end-point and how soon this end-point could be reached.

We will assume that our observer absolutely wants the white pieces to win and each thread is evaluated with respect to this desire. We therefore evaluate moves that are good for white as positive, and those good for black as negative.

With this setup, we can now simulate the suspense in a chess position with our narrative thread-based model of conflict-based suspense.

3.3.1 Applying our algorithm to the Réti study

According to the suspense algorithm in Doust (2015), after the telling of the nth story event, we calculate the suspense as a function of the *Imminence*$_n(Z)$, *Foregroundedness*$_n(Z)$, *Confidence*$_n(Z)$ and *Importance*$_n(Z)$ of each ac-

Proceedings of the 3rd Workshop on Computational Creativity and Natural Language Generation, pages 26–33,
Tilburg, November 2018. ©2018 Association for Computational Linguistics

tive narrative thread Z after story event n:

$$\begin{aligned}\text{Suspense}_n(Z) = \quad & \text{Imminence}_n(Z) \\ & \times \text{Importance}_n(Z) \\ & \times \text{Foregroundedness}_n(Z) \\ & \times \text{Confidence}_n(Z)\end{aligned} \quad (1)$$

Of course, some threads are more important than others and will have a bigger effect on suspense. The *Importance* of each narrative thread is equivalent to the predicted degree of positive or negative appraisal of the storyworld situation that the observer would have, were Z to succeed. The Importance values given here are based on standard chess practice that uses relative values of the pieces to evaluate board positions. Thus, if the white pawn queens at the endpoint of a thread, then this will give a value of $+8$ to that thread, because the value of a queen is 8 and the observer supports white.

In a standard chess game, the *Confidence* variable will always be equal to 1, as there are no hidden or untold moves.

As for the *Foregroundedness* variable, in previous work, we used a decay factor of 0.88 to determine the rate at which threads decay in importance when they are not explicitly evoked in a story step. However, in this first approach, we will ignore this variable, that is, we will ignore any memory effects and consider its value as always equal to 1.

Thus, the suspense contribution of a thread will depend only on its *Importance* and its *Imminence*.

3.3.2 Imminence

At a given point in the telling of the story, each active narrative thread Z generates two values for Imminence.

Completion Imminence is related to the number of moves in Z still to be played for it to be completed or to 'succeed'. For the starting position of the chess board above, the thread corresponding to the black pawn advancing to queen has a completion imminence of 4. In other words, it will take this thread 4 steps to complete.

Interruption Imminence is related to the smallest number of steps still to be played in some other thread before a step can be occur which interrupts Z by disallowing one of its steps[3]. The question to ask is: "How soon can this thread be interrupted?".

[3]In the case where no thread can interrupt Z, the Interruption Imminence of Z is taken as zero.

In the case of our black pawn thread, the interruption imminence is 3, as the pawn's moves can only be interrupted by the white king taking it and this requires 3 steps.

We use the definition in Doust (2015) of the Total Imminence$_n(Z)$ of a narrative thread Z after the nth event in the story:

$$\text{Total Imminence} = \rho\frac{1}{H} + (1-\rho)\frac{1}{R} \quad (2)$$

where H is the number of events to the completion of Z and R is the minimum number of events before an event in some other narrative thread could be told which would disallow some untold event in Z. The factor ρ is used to vary the relative weighting of these two imminence effects. Experimentation with the implementation of our model (see Doust (2015)) led us to choose $\rho = 0.7$, in effect boosting the relative effect of *Completion imminence* over *Interruption Imminence.*

3.3.3 Overall step-by-step suspense value

Finally we use a heuristic to combine all these individual narrative thread suspense values and produce the *global* suspense level at each moment in the story. Our method is to assume that it is the thread with the *highest suspense value* that is the one responsible for the story's evoked suspense at that point and we take this thread's contribution as equivalent to the overall suspense level of the narrative at that point in the story. Different threads will have the most important effect on suspense at different points in the story.

We can now apply our algorithm to calculate values for the suspense inherent at any point in this chess endgame.

3.3.4 Starting position

We first represent the starting positions of the pieces on the board: [White King h8, Black pawn h5, White Pawn c6, Black King a6]. Of course, in this starting position, it seems likely that there will already be some suspense. We therefore consider that the following threads may already be active in the starting position:

- Black Pawn tries to queen
- White Pawn tries to queen
- Black King chases the White Pawn

The only piece to which we ascribe no active thread at the beginning is the White King. This

Proceedings of the 3rd Workshop on Computational Creativity and Natural Language Generation, pages 26–33,
Tilburg, November 2018.

first list of threads can be used to calculate the initial suspense levels.

3.3.5 Choosing a story

In the starting position of the study in question, it is White's move. Two options seem to present themselves:

- The White King tries (hopelessly) to move down the *column* to catch the Black Pawn and stop it from queening (h8-h7-h6-...)
- The White King tries to move along the *row* to get close to the White Pawn and protect it so that it can queen. (h8-g8-f8-...)

The interesting choice in chess terms, however, is for the White King to move to $g7$ which actually satisfies both of the above goals. (This choice also allows White to draw the game as shown in the standard analysis of the study.)

We will therefore first examine a sequence of moves that starts with this move. The particular 'chess story' of (necessarily) alternating white and black 'events' we will consider is the following:

- W.King moves diagonally to g7, B.Pawn moves down
- W.King moves diagonally to f6, B.King moves next to white pawn
- W.King moves diagonally to e5, B.King takes white pawn
- W.King moves to f4 towards the B.Pawn, B.Pawn moves down
- W.King moves to g3 next to the pawn, B.Pawn moves down
- W.King takes the B.Pawn

Now after each move, we can update the completion and interruption distances for each thread ands obtain a prediction of the overall suspense level at that point in the 'story'.

3.4 Suspense predictions

We show the suspense predictions given by our algorithm in Figure 3. The figure also shows the contributions from some individual threads to the overall value.

To show some of the potential of our approach, we show the suspense profiles of two different 'chess stories' that could be told in this position.

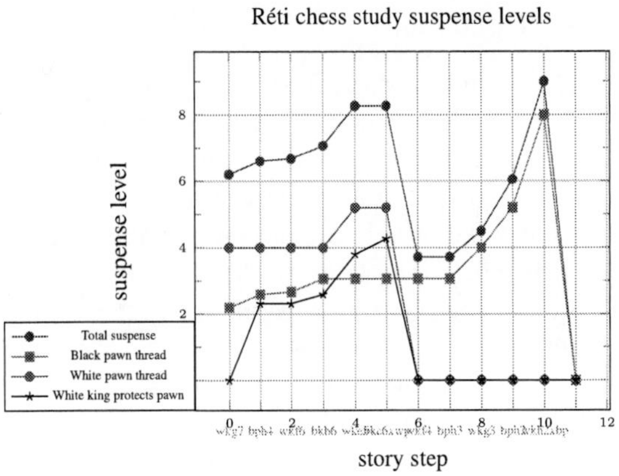

Figure 3: Suspense levels for Réti chess study

In Figure 4, we show the suspense levels for the story where the White King moves towards the White Pawn and protects it as it advances and queens: *wkg7,bph4,wkf6,bph3,wke6,bph2,wkd6,bph1q,wpc7*.

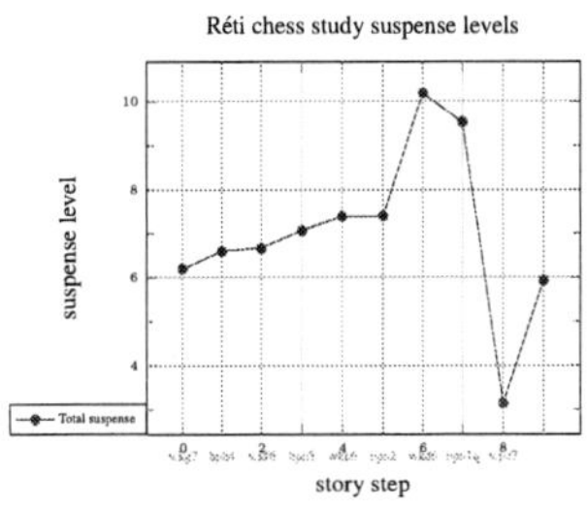

Figure 4: Suspense levels for "white king helps white pawn to queen"

In Figure 5, we show the suspense levels for the story where the White King merely tries to catch the Black Pawn as the Black Pawn moves down the board and queens: *wkh7,bph4,wkh6,bph3,wkh5,bph2,wkh4,bph1q*.

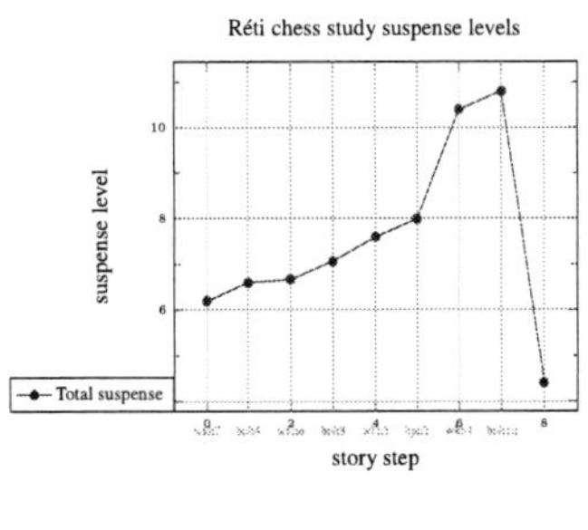

Figure 5: Suspense levels for "white king chases black pawn"

Proceedings of the 3rd Workshop on Computational Creativity and Natural Language Generation, pages 26–33,
Tilburg, November 2018. ©2018 Association for Computational Linguistics

4 Discussion

Chess studies are interesting for our purposes in that they are specifically designed to be surprising to the observer of the moves. This paper explores the possibility that at least one aspect of what makes a series of chess moves interesting is their ability to evoke story-like scenarios and more specifically generate suspense, surprise and curiosity.

The graph of suspense levels (Figure 3) clearly shows the switch in the pieces generating the suspense levels as the sequence of moves unfolds. We may consider therefore that a suspenseful chess match therefore will need different pieces to carry out the 'suspense creation' as the match progresses.

The design choices made for the present paper (see Section 1.1) align better with the approach to telling the story of a chess game followed in Delatorre and Gervás (2014), in the sense that the story considered is based on a perception of the complete chess board and the moves that take place over it. The alternative described – but not followed in this paper – where the story of the game is told in terms of partial views by certain pieces aligns better with the approach followed in Gervás (2014).

The model of suspense applied in this paper differs from others in the literature in that it is based on the interaction between a set of possible narrative threads as inferred by the reader from the partially told story. Other approaches do not consider this narrative level of suspense and focus more on the construction of possible plans for a given character (usually aimed at its survival in the face of danger).

5 Conclusions and Future Work

A further point is that it should be possible to calculate the suspensefulness of different move options and potentially to choose those options that produce the most suspense. Such an approach could be used as part of a system generating potential narrative sequences and then evaluating them for their suspensefulness in order to choose among them the most entertaining options.

Lastly, challenging though it may be, the predictions that this model makes need to be tested empirically for a range of participants. A factor that may be difficult to account for is the varying chess ability of the participants. Typically, in the study above, for example, as soon as it becomes clear to a reasonable chess player that the Black Pawn will be captured, then arguably there is no more suspense left in the game. This in itself points to further work on defining suspense for a specific player profile. One way to approach this would be to place different sized event horizons for the different players: experienced players would be able to see several moves ahead, beginners much fewer. These different levels of awareness may then generate predictably different suspense experiences.

References

W.F. Brewer and E.H. Lichtenstein. 1982. Stories are to entertain: A structural-affect theory of stories. *Journal of Pragmatics*, 6(5-6):473–486.

Marc Cavazza and Fred Charles. 2005. Dialogue Generation in Character-based Interactive Storytelling. *AAAI, AIIDE2005,*, pages 21–26.

Yun-Gyung Cheong and R Michael Young. 2015. Suspenser: A story generation system for suspense. *IEEE Transactions on Computational Intelligence and AI in Games*, 7(1):39–52.

Pablo Delatorre and Barbara Arfè. 2015. Modulare la suspense del lettore attraverso un modelo computazionale. In *XXVIII Congresso Nazionale Sezione di Psicologia dello sviluppo e dell'educazione.*

Pablo Delatorre, Barbara Arfè, Pablo Gervás, and Manuel Palomo-Duarte. 2016. A component-based architecture for suspense modelling. In *Proceedings of AISB 2016's Third International Symposium on Computational Creativity (CC2016).*

Pablo Delatorre and Pablo Gervás. 2014. Un modelo para la evaluación de la narrativa basada en partidas de ajedrez. In *Proceedings of the 1st Congreso de la Sociedad Española para las Ciencias del Videojuego (CoSECiVi 2014).* CEUR Workshop Proceedings, CEUR Workshop Proceedings.

Richard Doust. 2015. *A domain-independent model of suspense in narrative.* Ph.D. thesis, The Open University.

Richard Doust. 2017. A fundamental element for narrative parsing. *6th International Workshop on Computational Creativity, Concept Invention, and General Intelligence. Madrid, December 15th 2017.*

Richard Doust and Paul Piwek. 2017. A model of suspense for narrative generation. In *Proceedings of the 10th International Conference on Natural Language Generation*, pages 178–187.

Mark Dvoretsky. 2011. *Dvoretsky's endgame manual.* SCB Distributors.

P. Gervás. 2018a. Storifying observed events: Could i dress this up as a story? In *5th AISB Symposium on Computational Creativity*, University of Liverpool, UK. AISB, AISB.

Pablo Gervás. 2014. Composing narrative discourse for stories of many characters: a case study over a chess game. *Literary and Linguistic Computing*, 29(4).

Pablo Gervás. 2018b. Targeted storyfying: Creating stories about particular events. In *Ninth International Conference on Computational Creativity, ICCC 2018*, Salamanca, Spain. Association of Computational Creativity, Association of Computational Creativity.

Proceedings of the 3rd Workshop on Computational Creativity and Natural Language Generation, pages 26–33, Tilburg, November 2018.

Generating Stories Using Role-playing Games and Simulated Human-like Conversational Dynamics

Alan Tapscott
alan.tapscott@ucm.es

Carlos León
cleon@ucm.es

Pablo Gervás
pgervas@ucm.es

Facultad de Informática
Universidad Complutense de Madrid

Abstract

Tabletop role-playing games (RPGs) have a well-tested history of making possible the improvisation of a story through the players' interactions. Adapting these human dynamics and game setting and mechanics could represent a new and fertile approach to computational story generation. In this paper we introduce a story generation system that recreates the player interaction sequence that takes place in a tabletop role-playing game (essentially a human storyteller and a player character conversation). We then process these interactions to render a story following the rules and using the knowledge base from a popular RPG. Finally, we control parameters present in the narrative RPG ruleset to tweak the resulting story, such as the presence of mental, physical and social challenges, as well as the amount of protagonism that each player has.

1 Introduction

Role-playing games (RPGs) are a plausible model for narrative. They are a successful creative exercise in which the interaction between the players facilitates the emergence of a story. Their jump into the digital media represents one of the few successful forms of interactive narrative (Tychsen, 2006). This improvised human social interaction happens naturally, albeit constrained by the rules and setting of the game. Despite the pressure of keeping the game rhythm and the chaotic nature of improvisation, the resulting stories are coherent enough for being recorded in multiple forms of media. Not only some popular books and characters have been based on real RPG game sessions that took place at some point, but lately we have how there is an audience for online videos and podcasts that record live RPGs.

Using RPGs for story management or generation is not a new idea. For instance there is work detailing the usage of a game master (GM) story facilitator (Aylett, 1999), or automating story orchestration just like a GM would (Graham et al., 2012). Other attempts include implementing a belief-desire-intent system into a computer game to perform as a GM (Luong et al., 2017) or adapting game mastering laws for interactive storytelling (Peinado and Gervas, 2004). Similarly, simulating with agents to drive the generation is not unheard-of, for instance there have been attempts that build upon conversational threads for virtual actors for interactive digital storytelling (Spierling et al., 2006) or the development and creation of characters with feelings and personalities (Curry and O'Shea, 2012). Also, some approaches explore the potential of agent-based systems, such as managing the interaction of human users with computer-controlled agents (Riedl et al., 2003), system that use autonomous believable character agents to augment a story world simulation (Riedl and Stern, 2006) a modular microservice-oriented story stage ecosystem (Concepción et al., 2018) or an implementation of agents to behave according to the scripts via automated tuning of goal parameters (Si et al., 2005). Despite the rich existing attempts to use RPGs for story generation, we believe there's still potential in them to be tapped into.

In this approach, we explore RPG-based story generation. However, instead of focusing on the rules driving the game, we propose to abstract one level and examine the interaction, the *conversation* itself as a source of narrative content. By simulating the human interactions that take place during a RPG session and implementing a game's ruleset and knowledge base derived from its setting we

Proceedings of the 3rd Workshop on Computational Creativity and Natural Language Generation, pages 34–42,
Tilburg, November 2018.

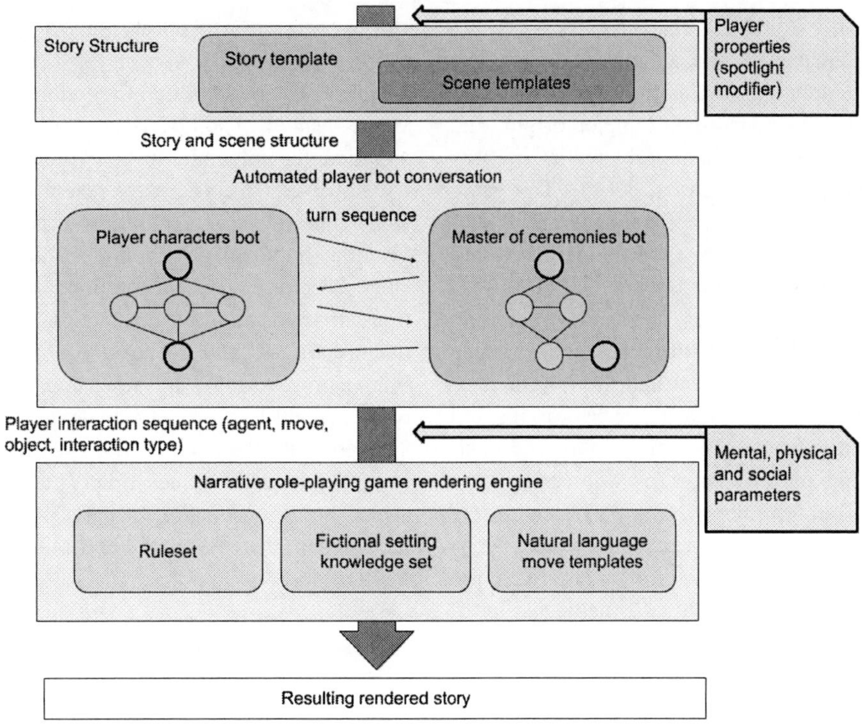

Figure 1: Story Generator structure

can generate stories similar to the ones created in a RPG session. To our best knowledge, this focus on *conversational dynamics* has not yet been exploited for creative processes in a computational system.

2 RPG-based Story Generation from Players' Conversational Dynamics

We propose to generate stories using a sequence of human-like interactions (mimicking conversation dynamics that happen in a RPG tabletop experience), a RPG ruleset (providing the base structure and dynamics) and the RPGs fictional setting knowledge base (used to fill and enrich the generated skeleton structures with the desired background and aesthetics). The artifacts provided by the generator should resemble the kind of stories the creators of the game had in mind while also being a human-like story.

The presented solution to story generation has the following key contributions:

- The conversation automation is RPG implementation-agnostic. Using distinct RPGs would produce distinct stories.
- Control over certain narrative aspects (such as character protagonism or threat types) thanks to the parameters included by narrative games.
- Streamlining of certain tasks of RPGs that typically require additional effort, such as number upkeeping, balancing magnitudes and distributing resources.

The following modules constitute the proposed story generator. Their configuration can be seen in Figure 1.

- A story structure that includes a story template containing scene templates that serves as the backbone of the story to provide context to the player interactions
- Automated player bot agents that interact with each other and produce a sequence of abstract interactions meant to resemble human conversation dynamics
- A rendering engine capable of processing abstract interactions and generate template-based natural language

2.1 RPGs: from Adventure simulation to Open Ended Narrative Improvisation

Our first concern would be to pick a RPG to base our generator on. Role-playing games are

Proceedings of the 3rd Workshop on Computational Creativity and Natural Language Generation, pages 34–42,
Tilburg, November 2018. ©2018 Association for Computational Linguistics

about playing a specific character, trying to behave as someone else in a fictional, interactive story. The popularity of their video game adaptations have obfuscated their tabletop origins and made their distinction more problematic(Hitchens and Drachen, 2009; Tychsen, 2006). The genre became popular with the Dungeons and Dragons (Gygax and Arneson, 1974) boom in the seventies. These early iterations were focused on simulating fantasy adventures, and were structurally and mechanically close to the simulation wargame hobby. One of the players had the role of dungeon master, or game master. She was responsible for introducing the setting, story and challenges to the player characters, who each played the role of an adventurer. The player characters went through the trials presented by the GM to reach the ultimate reward. From a narrative point of view, the story was almost cosmetic, and introducing the games setting's own tropes, aesthetic and ambience without much impact in the game's mechanics.

Over time, some new role-playing games introduced more flexible rulesets to put emphasis on the story. Vampire the Masquerade (Rein-Hagen, 1991) was the first game to have the golden rule, that is, to explicitly empower the Storyteller (equivalent to the GM) to modify any aspect of the game that helps in telling the story she wants to. Also, it encouraged the Storyteller to focus less in the mechanical challenge and more in the emerging story. It de-emphasized the antagonism between GM and player characters (PCs) and it encouraged their collaboration to create a story together. The resulting family of RPG games, often denominated narrative games, presents mechanics and dynamics that are meant to propitiate the emergence of a story through a human conversation. Some of the latest most proposals embrace an even more free and dynamic view of role-playing games, proposing an experience close to free-form theatrical improvisations, going as far as to removing the figure of the GM, eliminating the player asymmetry, embracing a more democratic and creative approach. Therefore, we are interested in two elements found in narrative RPGs: a discrete ruleset meant to mediate player interactions and a knowledge base with fictional setting-specific story elements and tropes.

We chose the Apocalypse World (D. Vincent Baker and Baker, 2010) (AW) ruleset to base our story generator on. Apocalypse World introduced the Powered by the Apocalypse (PbTA) engine, a ruleset that was built and functions in an innovative fashion. The PbTA game system has been significantly influential in the whole RPG industry, however we chose it for several specific reasons. The ruleset is focused on narrative improvisation, reducing the importance of pre-session story structuring and preparation. Most interactions are based on action abstractions called moves that are abstract and leave room for interpretation in meaning, causality and story impact. It also includes actual lists of elements and parameters to auto generate the story world, such as locations, objects, character names, motivations and their typical behavior. Finally, the post-apocalyptic aesthetic favors less populated and minimalist story worlds.

2.2 Input parameters and effect

We have included some input parameters that can provide control over the story. In a tabletop RPG experience, generally speaking, it is better if all player characters have a similar window of time to play their characters. The MC (AW's denomination for the GM role) is generally responsible of this. In our approach, we can limit every player character's moves, and by extension, how much presence they end up having in the final story. To do so, we introduce the *spotlight* metric. Player character bots accumulate spotlight points when either they are the agent or object of a move. Spotlight points will be then used to weight the random function used to determine what player characters are included in a scene and what player characters are either the agent or object of a move. As result, by default all player characters should be featured in a similar measure in the story. Since player bots do not care about their attention, if we desire to give more visibility to a certain player character, we can simply add a multiplier that reduces the amount of spotlight point that she earns. This metric can be used to establish a clear protagonist or to introduce secondary or even deuteragonist characters.

Our system is naive when choosing what moves to assign to what interaction beyond the action/reply/interference/end dynamics. Certain moves evoke certain story types, even within the base theme and mood of AW stories. A required element can be retrieved by either seduc-

Proceedings of the 3rd Workshop on Computational Creativity and Natural Language Generation, pages 34–42,
Tilburg, November 2018.

ing/manipulating or by doing battle, however the resulting story will be quite different. To adapt this, we resort to the Mental, Physical and Social ratings (MPS) introduced in the SAS storytelling adventure system developed by White Wolf Inc (Webb and Hindmarch, 2008). SAS was meant to be a universal system for writing tabletop RPG adventures, and the MPS was used to rate narrative scenes in terms of mental physical and social challenge. The stories published using the SAS system had a global MPS rating and a scene MPS rating. Since our generated story structure also has these two levels, we quantified all the implemented moves with an MPS rating, allowing us to prejudice their incidences to achieve scenes and stories that fulfill a certain MPS criteria. This way we can either obtain stories with balanced mental, physical and social moves, or stories that favor one of the three magnitudes.

2.3 Scene and Story Templates

Our next concern would be to provide the generator with a basic structure or framework to build the story upon. While AW is focused on moves and the player conversation, it is vague in its discussion on the overall story structure. It does suggest framing the action in scenes, each involving the MC and some PCs. From a structural perspective, our system's story model is composed by scenes. Both, the story and the scenes follow a specific template that requires certain conditions to end. For the story, the implemented template is meant to represent a journey, in which the protagonists are moving to reach a specific location. For every scene, the only implemented template requires the player characters to obtain a specific element to ensure their survival. When the scene is generated, the missing element is assigned to a random threat. Once any player character does any move targeted against the threat that possesses the required element, she will automatically obtain the element and the scene will be marked as ready to finish. The nature of the move or player interaction that results in the retrieval of the missing element is not relevant for the system's functioning.

Therefore, the generated story should contain a finite sequence of scenes in which the player characters obtain elements they need to survive until they reach their final destination. The final destination and the location for every scene will be randomly generated using lists provided in the

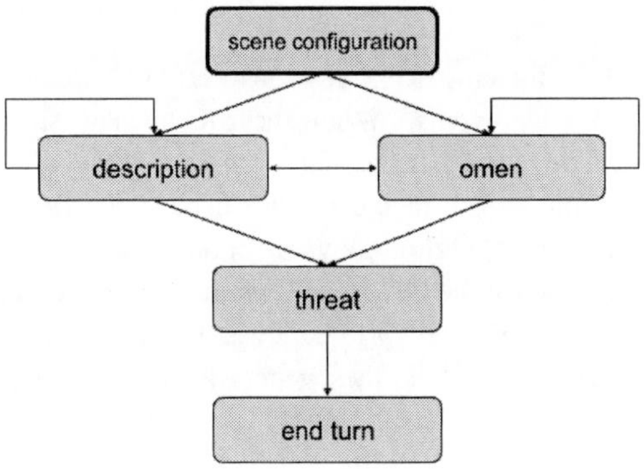

Figure 2: MC Interaction State Diagram

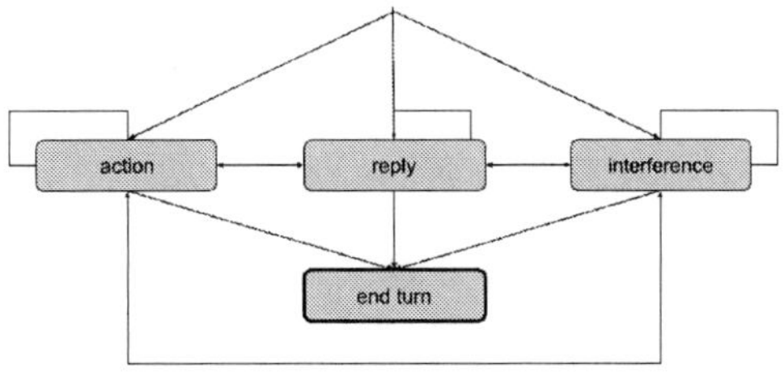

Figure 3: PCs Interaction State Diagram

AW fictional setting. Also, the required elements, scenery elements, the present PCs and the present threats will also be randomly generated from the setting knowledge base provided by AW. In our implemented prototype, we introduced 4 PC playbooks, 2 threat types and 23 survival resources (all extracted from the AW rules) as well as 12 location names and 31 scenery elements (extracted from the AW provided examples and recommended media).

2.4 Master of Ceremonies and Player Character Conversational Interactions

The next relevant module, would be the player conversation interactions simulator. In a tabletop RPG, specially in the ones that take place in narrative games, the gameplay is essentially a conversation between the players that involves certain game mechanics. For the purpose of our simulator, we need to simulate this conversation dynamics between the actual players by implementing automated bots that behave in a similar way. The resulting interaction sequence should resemble that one of a real tabletop RPG session. Note that at this stage we are not trying to synthesize the content the interactions beyond their abstract representation, this will be done at a later stage (natural

Proceedings of the 3rd Workshop on Computational Creativity and Natural Language Generation, pages 34–42,
Tilburg, November 2018. ©2018 Association for Computational Linguistics

language rendering).

In a tabletop RPG session there are two very distinctive events. When the MC speaks, she is behaving like a storyteller, configuring the whole fictional world, including the scenery and threats while excluding the playable characters. She sets the stage for the PCs to act or reacts to the PCs actions making the world believable and interactive. When the PCs talk, they generally start a multiple participant conversation while driving the plot forward with their actions. Our system distinguishes these two stages of the player interaction and will alternate between the MC and the PCs turn. Every turn will include one or more interactions. The MC turn, will include the following possible interactions (presented in Figure 2):

1. scene configuration: Present the context to the PCs, providing details of the location and explaining the goal of the scene. This is always the first interaction in a scene and happens once per scene.
2. description: Detail the ambience and mood of the scene. Evoke the target mood and theme.
3. threat: Use a threat (through the environment or a non player character) to provoke some sort of crisis.
4. end turn: Finish the current MC turn

On the other hand, on the player characters turn, they have the following available interactions (Presented in Figure 3):

1. action: An agent performs a general purpose move on any target.
2. reply: The target of the last move replies with another move targeting the last move's agent. The reply move can be targeted to either a PC character or a MC threat.
3. interference: Some third party agent uninvolved in the last move interrupts with another move targeting the last move's agent or object.
4. end turn: Finish the current PCs turn

The system uses a random number generator to decide the sequence of interactions that takes place in each of the alternating turns. The probabilities were assigned arbitrarily. Note that only the master of ceremonies player acts during her turn, but all player characters can potentially act during their turn. The decision to make every turn exclusive to either the MC or the PCs, not allowing to interleave each others' interactions into a hybrid turn, was based in our informal observations of real RPG games. MCs tend to drag, creating monologues to configure the scene while PCs tend to interrupt and cooperate with each other to answer the MCs interventions. This arbitrary design decision is addressed more in depth in the discussion section. Next we introduce a couple of exemplified MC and PCs turns:

The MC begins her turn with a **scene configuration** interaction, then a **description** and then a **threat** aimed at player 1. Finally she **ends** the MC turn. After the MC turn and during the PCs turn, player 1 initiates with a reflexive **action**, then adds a follow up **action** targeting player 2. Then player 2 **replies** with another action directed at player 1. Finally, player 3 steps in and **interferes**, targeting player 2 with her action. The PCs turn could **end** here. In the following MC turn, since we're still in the same scene, the MC skips the scene configuration, adds two **omen** interactions and one **threat** before **ending** her turn. In the second PCs turn, player 1 starts with an **action** interaction, followed by a **reply** to him by player 2 and an **ending** interaction. After this, the turn would switch back to the MC, and so on until the scene is over. This process would be repeated until the story template runs out of scenes.

2.5 Moves, Playbooks and Threats

In this module, we convert the previous abstract conversational interactions into actual entities that make sense in the context of the story world, moves. AW and the PbTA game system introduce the flexible concept of moves. A move is a generalization of a set of actions performed by an agent entity to an object entity, simplifying their mechanical effects while allowing a broad spectrum of expression. Some are meant to target the environment (such as read a situation), some are reactive (such as act under pressure) and some only make sense as interruptions (such as interrupting some action). The MC is responsible for working with the players to determine what moves are being performed, triggering their emergence during the unfolding interaction. The game suggests not to constraint player interaction to the available moves, but to adapt the moves to the player natural behavior. For instance, if a player wants to analyze something, she might be *reading a sitch.* If she wants to start a fight, she might be *doing battle.* PBTA games are meant to reflect heavily genre-specific tropes, so if the game was based on

Proceedings of the 3rd Workshop on Computational Creativity and Natural Language Generation, pages 34–42, Tilburg, November 2018.

pulp noir novels, the player might be *investigating a scene*, or *starting a street brawl*. In the case of Apocalypse World, the whole ruleset was built to recreate apocalyptic stories such as the ones found in films of the like of Mad Max, The Road or The Stand.

In AW players are forced to pick a playbook, a character write up closely attached to the game's theme and aesthetic (e.g the driver, the exterminator or the biker). Each player may use general moves and specific moves to her playbook. All character can *read a sitch* or *go aggro*, but only the angel can perform a *healing touch*. Also, every playbook asks the player to customize certain parameters such as the character name, description or link to other characters, always offering a limited set of options. The MC does not pick a playbook, however the rules provide her with moves and threats. The moves are less specific than the PCs ones, they still outline the general principles and behavior expected from the MC player. They also encourage story beats expected from a post-apocalyptic fiction piece. Most involve depicting the fictional world, its elements and denizens, however, some involve well-defined threats. Threats are created from a limited pool contained in the game's rules such as grotesques or warlords (D. Vincent Baker and Baker, 2010, p. 138), and have specific moves associated that reflect their nature.

Our generator creates a character for every player, picking the necessary parameters from the provided set. Also, creates a pool of Threats for the MC to use. The resulting set of generated elements, will define the moves that will be possible during the simulated game session, as well as most of their potential actors and objects.

2.6 Natural Language Rendering

The last module of our system is concerned with transforming moves into natural language that makes sense to the reader. The module is agnostic of the story structure configuration and is merely concerned with the conversion from the moves into story sentences. Since Moves are abstractions that make sense in the context of a specific kind of story, they could be written in many permutations of natural language. More so, the context can influence a great deal what write ups make or not make sense for a specific move. Beyond the basic configuration of agent/object/move, many factors can potentially influence the resulting text. For the purpose of our generator, we have paired every move with an array of text templates to be filled with the domain-specific data needed for their rendering. For instance, the text templates for *read a sitch* have the following format:

{agent} observes thoroughly the {location_name}, paying special attention to the {scene.location.get_elements(random(1,3))}

Which once filled with the appropriate data, could be transformed into natural language:

Abondo observes thoroughly the cave, paying special attention to the maggots and the tubercules

The parameters get filled dynamically when using interactions with their context. The template will just replace the agent, scene location and scene location elements with the right data from the story template, scene template and interaction from the sequence. With the sequence of interactions that we generated in the previous section, our next step is to pair each interaction with a move. By pairing moves with player conversational interactions, we translate a sequence of abstract interactions into a series of abstract moves with a text representation that make sense in the context of a post-apocalyptic story. This was done in the following way for the player character moves:

1. action move: Any move that is not explicitly written as a reply or interference and requires a character object.
2. reply move: Any move, regardless of it was written as a reply or not, that does require a character object and was not written as an interference.
3. interference move: Any move, regardless of it was written as an interference or not, that does require a character object and was not written as a reply.

For the MC, this proved to be more challenging. Most of the moves enunciated were highly abstract or required complex natural language formulation we were not capable of generating in the relevant module. We introduced some base moves that followed the principles enunciated for the MC (scene configurations, descriptions and omens) while implementing the ones included in the rules that our approach was capable of (threats):

1. scene configuration: We generate a text detailing the location for the scene and what player and non player characters are present.
2. description: We generate a short sentence de-

Proceedings of the 3rd Workshop on Computational Creativity and Natural Language Generation, pages 34–42, Tilburg, November 2018. ©2018 Association for Computational Linguistics

scribing the scenery and some of its elements.

3. omen: We generate a description for a location that is not the one featured in the scene.
4. threat: These are given a more specific template, mostly involving non player characters that are hostile to the PCs.

One of the main issues with the overall approach, is that since the coupling between player interactions and moves is completely random, the resulting text might seem quite incoherent. Adding a motive of some sort is fundamental so the reader can get some notions of causality from the reading experience. For this purpose, we rely on several elements. First, the scene template (that involves recovering a missing element) provides a clear motive for the move. In this case, we would complement the result with a proper suffix: ***p1*** *does something to* ***threat1****, recovering the* ***missing element****.* Another motive we use, are player history relations. All of AW's playbooks have player establish previous history between them. Our generator creates these relationships and uses them to expand the first move rendering between the relevant players: ***p1*** *manipulates* ***p2****.* ***p1*** *and* ***p2 have history*** *together.* The last element we use are the impulses of threats. AW threats not only have moves, but also an impulse. The impulse is meant to be used as the driving force for the threat to act, and is antagonistic to the players. Using the impulse, we expand the renderings of any threat's move: ***threat1*** *does something to* ***p1*** *because she has an* ***impulse****.* The implemented prototype had 17 PC moves and 19 MC moves extracted from the AW rules, each with two distinct natural language templates. These templates resorted to auxiliary lists of 12 location names, 31 location elements, 100 general adjectives, 78 personality adjectives (all extracted from the AW examples and recommended media as well as an arbitrary word corpus) and 24 threat motivations (extracted from the AW rules).

3 Example

This section has a step by step execution of the story generator, illustrating the detailed process to construct a scene using our approach.

Our initial setup will involve four players. We gave all the same spotlight rating, except for p2 who will have a spotlight index of 4 to become the protagonist. MPS wise, we gave the magnitudes values of 0.25, 0 and 1. We want a social story with little physicality and a few mental interactions.

- players: p1, p2, p3 and p4
- playbooks: p1 plays Enoughto-eat the artist, p2 plays Kettle the angel, p3 plays Preen the exterminator and p4 plays III the Driver

Our story template will be the journey, which requires a destination.

Story template

- locations: The Sick Desert, the Good Mountain, the Bad Cave, the Depression
- destination: The Good Mountain

Scene template

- location: the Bad Cave
- missing resource: meat
- player characters: Enoughto-eat the artist, Kettle the angel and Preen the exterminator
- threats: Dremmer the masochist aberrant and Krin the warlord
- target: Krin has the meat

Once the templates have been filled, we can now start to generate the conversation interactions. Conversation interaction sequences are made of tuples of agent, move, object and interaction type.

We begin with the first MC turn

- `(mc, scene_conf,)‘`
- `(mc, omen, sick desert)`
- `(mc, description, bad cave)`
- `(mc, threat, p2)`
- `(mc, end,)`

Next we run the first PCs turn. Since p2 has a high spotlight index, she is more likely to be either the agent or object of most interactions.

- `(p2, reply, MC)`
- `(p2, action, MC)`
- `(p1, interference, p2)`
- `(p3, action, bad cave)`
- `(, end, )`

At this point, we would continue generating interactions until an arbitrary condition set in the template is met (for instance, after three turns for each). Social moves are more likely to be picked when converting the interactions into moves and physical move will be introduced if possible (MPS magnitudes were set to favor social and neglect physical). We will skip ahead to the rendering process.

- *Enoughto-eat, Kettle and Preen arrive to the Bad Cave searching for meat. Dremmer and Krin are dwelling there. Krin has the meat they need.*

Proceedings of the 3rd Workshop on Computational Creativity and Natural Language Generation, pages 34–42,
Tilburg, November 2018.

- *Somewhere out there, there's a Sick Desert with noise and pain.*
- *The oil of the Bad Cave is common and bitter.*
- *Dremmer guides Kettle to the cave's sand.*
- *Kettle manipulates Dremmer with subtlety.*
- *Kettle uses her healing touch with Krin, obtaining the meat from him.*
- *Enoughto-eat shows some of her skin to Kettle.*
- *Preen reads the sitch in the cave, noticing the sand and the bullets.*

We have skipped several sentences, such as the rendering of the story introduction that explains the overall story objective (complete the journey), as well as the scene and story conclusion. While the results are not very specific and the rendering leaves room for interpretation, however the usage of elements from the game's setting might help readers (specially those familiar with the genre) in finding the results consistent and coherent.

4 Discussion

The presented approach relies on the emergence of sense by combining structures and knowledge from a role-playing game. This implies that the resulting stories will always be conditioned by the RPG used to convert the player interactions into moves or any other abstraction meant for the story world. This might be mitigated by combining rules and knowledge from multiple RPGs. It remains to be seen how scalable would be this approach with all the potential problems of conceptual overlapping and compromised consistency and coherence. Also, rigid text templates such as the ones we have used will quickly be spotted by any reader upon certain repetition. The rendering of moves may be improved by introducing a more complex grammar, templates parsed from related media or results enriched with predictive or machine learning approaches.

The random functions used to move between user interactions, generate names for items, traits and locations and the selection of a language template for a move follow completely arbitrary distributions based on our informal observations. As previously mentioned, we've separated the MC and PCs turn based on our intuition and informal observations arbitrarily. This is clearly a direction for future work. In order to inform the system's many choices, we might require extensive field work, analyzing real RPG sessions or even other related fictional media. The same criticism is applicable to the story and scene templates, which were designed after some of the most classic structuralist perspectives (a hero's journey that includes the acquisition of competences and the ultimate sanction).

The general goal of the generation system is to fulfill the story and scene template conditions (reach the final destination and obtain the missing elements). A common criticism to generative systems with goals is that the character and user goals are not the same. Certainly, AW states clearly that the goal is to have fun and build a story. While we acknowledge this criticism, we also argue that the failure to reach these conditions still constitutes an interesting story. Ultimately, having a simulated conversational layer (in which the goal is to entertain its participants) and a story logical layer (in which the goal is to complete character objectives) coexisting in our approach might make possible to achieve a certain balance between both objectives.

Overall, albeit the resulting text does not reflect a human quality-like result, the current text artifacts could be used to structure plots for trope-intensive genre fiction or as inspirational material.

5 Conclusions

We have described an original story generation system based on the character and game master conversation dynamics in a RPG game. We have illustrated how the implementation of the system allows tweaking player protagonism and the presence of mental/physical and social challenges. We have shown a model for shifting the focus from the pure game universe to the interactive game itself, explicitly controlling aspects such as the protagonism and the presence of mental, physical and social challenges. This enriches the generation by adding a new set of structures not present in the story world itself.

While there is plenty of room for improvement, the present approach has show how to address meta-narrative aspects and apply them into a story generation. Our present implementation constructs the final story by relying on template-based knowledge, but we believe the general model (i.e. focusing on the interaction) can be applied to other systems.

Proceedings of the 3rd Workshop on Computational Creativity and Natural Language Generation, pages 34–42,
Tilburg, November 2018. ©2018 Association for Computational Linguistics

References

Ruth Aylett. 1999. Narrative in Virtual Environments - Towards Emergent Narrative. In *AAAI fall symposium on narrative intelligence*.

Eugenio Concepción, Pablo Gervás, and Méndez Gonzalo. 2018. INES: A reconstruction of the Charade storytelling system using the Afanasyev Framework. In *Proceedings of the Ninth International Conference on Computational Creativity (ICCC 2018)*.

Collette Curry and James D O'Shea. 2012. The Implementation of a Story Telling Chatbot. In *New Directions in Agent Research*. Nakanishiya Shuppan. http://nimbusvault.net/publications/koala/assr/29.html.

D. Vincent Baker and Meguey Baker. 2010. *Apocalypse World*. 2 edition.

T. C. Nicholas Graham, Quentin Bellay, Irina Schumann, and Amir Sepasi. 2012. Toward game orchestration. In *Proceedings of the Sixth International Conference on Tangible, Embedded and Embodied Interaction - TEI '12*. ACM Press, New York, New York, USA, page 187. https://doi.org/10.1145/2148131.2148171.

Gary Gygax and Dave Arneson. 1974. *Dungeons and dragons*.

Michael Hitchens and Anders Drachen. 2009. The Many Faces of Role-Playing Games. Technical report.

Bao Luong, John Thangarajah, and Fabio Zambetta. 2017. A BDI Game Master Agent for Computer Role-Playing Games. *Computers in Entertainment* 15(1):1–16. https://doi.org/10.1145/2629700.

Federico Peinado and Pablo Gervas. 2004. Transferring game mastering laws to interactive digital storytelling. *Lecture notes in computer science* pages 48–54.

Mark Rein-Hagen. 1991. *Vampire the Masquerade*. White Wolf, Inc.

Mark Riedl, C. J. Saretto, and R. Michael Young. 2003. Managing interaction between users and agents in a multi-agent storytelling environment. In *Proceedings of the second international joint conference on Autonomous agents and multiagent systems - AAMAS '03*. ACM Press, New York, New York, USA, page 741. https://doi.org/10.1145/860575.860694.

Mark O. Riedl and Andrew Stern. 2006. Believable Agents and Intelligent Story Adaptation for Interactive Storytelling. In *International Conference on Technologies for Interactive Digital Storytelling and Entertainment*. Springer, Berlin, Heidelberg, pages 1–12.

Mei Si, Stacy C. Marsella, and David V. Pynadath. 2005. Thespian. In *Proceedings of the fourth international joint conference on Autonomous agents and multiagent systems - AAMAS '05*. ACM Press, New York, New York, USA, page 21. https://doi.org/10.1145/1082473.1082477.

Ulrike Spierling, Sebastian A. Weiß, and Wolfgang Müller. 2006. Towards Accessible Authoring Tools for Interactive Storytelling. Springer, Berlin, Heidelberg, pages 169–180.

Anders Tychsen. 2006. Role Playing Games-Comparative Analysis Across Two Media Platforms. Technical report.

Eddy Webb and Will Hindmarch. 2008. Storytelling adventure system. https://www.drivethrurpg.com/product/54404/Storytelling-Adventure-System-Guide.

Proceedings of the 3rd Workshop on Computational Creativity and Natural Language Generation, pages 34–42, Tilburg, November 2018.

Association for Computational Linguistics
209 N. Eighth Street
Stroudsburg, Pennsylvania 18360

ISBN 978-1-5108-7757-3
9 781510 877573

CURRAN ASSOCIATES INC.
proceedings.com